D1165241

ARCTIC
MEMORIES

ARCTIC MEMORIES

LIVING WITH THE INUIT

FRED BRUEMMER

KEY PORTER BOOKS

To all the Inuit who took me in,
and to Maud who took me back

Copyright © 1993 Fred Bruemmer

All rights reserved. No part of this work covered by the copyrights
hereon may be reproduced or used in any form or by any means –
graphic, electronic or mechanical, including photocopying,
recording, taping or information storage and retrieval systems –
without the prior written permission of the publisher, or, in case of
photocopying or other reprographic copying, without a licence
from the Canadian Reprography Collective.

Canadian Cataloguing in Publication Data

Bruemmer, Fred
    Arctic memories: living with the Inuit
Includes index.
ISBN 1-55013-461-2 hardcover
ISBN 1-55013-499-X paperback

1. Inuit - Canada.* I. Title.

E99.E7B78 1993   971'.004971   C93-093759-7

Key Porter Books Limited
70 The Esplanade
Toronto, Ontario
Canada M5E 1R2

Distributed in the United States of
America by:
National Book Network, Inc.
4720 Boston Way
Lanham, MD 20706

*Jessie Hakungak and
Karetak.*

*Page 1: George Hakungak,
Ekalun's son, wearing
bone goggles.*

*Page 2: Traveling over
flooded sea ice in the
summer.*

The publisher gratefully acknowledges the assistance of the Canada
Council and the Ontario Arts Council in the publication of this
work.

Design and page composition: Andrew Smith Graphics Inc.
Printed and bound in Italy ,

93 94 95 96 97 6 5 4 3 2 1

CONTENTS

Ooloopie Killiktee, the heart and soul of the camp at Kiijuak, Baffin Island, Canada.

INTRODUCTION

BEGINNINGS

WE TRAVELED FROM NOWHERE TO NOWHERE IN A WORLD ALL WHITE, eleven dogs, a long sled, a fur-clad Inuk and I. We had spent a week at the floe edge, the limit of landfast ice, and the hunting had been good. Jes had shot and harpooned eight seals. We had eaten well and our sled was heavy with meat — food for his family and dogs — and with seal pelts he would sell at the store.

We felt the coming of the storm. The air was still and oppressive. Gulls, screaming, flew toward the distant land. The sky turned leaden black. We should have left hours ago. But a pod of narwhals was feeding close to the floe edge; the eerie stillness was filled with the plosive "pooff," "pooff," "pooff" of their breathing. Small plumes of exhaled breath hung briefly in the icy air, and a few times we saw the gleaming ivory tusks of the males.

Jes wanted a whale. His entire hunter's spirit was focused on those whales, wishing them closer, closer. He was the perfect predator, quietly poised in total concentration, the ultimate Arctic hunter, as his people had been since the dawn of time. The whale meant food and life and glory, the primal thrill of being, and at that moment nothing else mattered.

A hunter at the floe edge.

While Jes's soul was in that strange mystic sphere that links the hunter to his prey, I sat apart and nursed my white man's worries. I had spent far too many years in the Arctic not to know that the coming storm would be hell, the trip home utter misery and, if the ice broke up, exceedingly dangerous. It was 60 miles (96 km) back to the village.

The storm struck, and Jes did not get his whale. He rose slowly, reluctantly. The tension seeped out of him and then he smiled a marvelously boyish smile, shrugged, and said: "*Ayornamat.* (It can't be helped.)" An Inuk does not rant and rave; his language has no swearwords. He does not rail against God or Nature, but simply accepts adversity. He does his best; the rest is fate.

We lashed the load upon the long pliant sled with utmost care, passing the bearded-seal thong back and forth, pulling it tight with all our strength. Jes called to the dogs. Normally they would have leapt into a joyous gallop. Now they moved without enthusiasm, their tails, usually cockily curled, drooping sadly. Like me, they feared the storm.

At first, brief lulls alternated with vicious gusts. Then the storm became steady and we traveled into a hissing, roaring avalanche of snow. The dogs hated it. The wind-lashed ice spicules hurt their eyes, and they tried to veer away from the wind. Jes beat them,

coaxed them, directed them. There was only snow, the screaming wind, and nothingness; we seemed suspended in time and space. But Jes was guided by *sastrugi,* snow ripples created by prevailing winds, and by the knowledge of a thousand trips since he had first gone to the floe edge as a small boy with his father.

We traveled for hours, our faces seared by the wind, our fur clothing plastered with snow. The ice changed, became rugged, hummocky. We were in a tidal zone, close to a coast. For a moment I saw a cliff and then it vanished again in the whirling white. Jes walked ahead now, leading the dogs through a maze of ice blocks. Near the base of the cliff he tied the dogs securely to a stone upon the ice. "Come," he said. We clambered up an incline, perhaps a beach in summertime, walked past a house-high rock, squeezed through a triangular hole between the rock and the cliff, and were suddenly in a spacious cave. Jes laughed, delighted by my amazement, the magician who has performed the perfect trick.

Jes unharnessed and tethered the dogs, then cut up a seal and fed them. They rolled into balls, noses tucked under bushy tails, and soon the snow covered them with an insulating blanket. I lugged our sled load into the cave, shook the snow out of the bedding furs and my clothing, and made supper: a big pot of seal meat boiled on a Primus stove.

After the elemental chaos of the storm, the cave felt calm and

A Polar Inuk of Greenland scouts the ice for seals in the early spring of 1971.

Jes Qujaukitsoq of the Polar Inuit hunts seals at the floe edge in 1971.

Inuit are a sharing people; a small girl at a camp on Fury and Hecla Strait gives food to her father.

secure. It had obviously served as sanctuary to other Arctic hunters for hundreds, perhaps thousands of years. In the back were low sleeping platforms of pebbles and flat stones. Soot streaks along the walls and roof showed where seal-oil lamps had burned and flared. The cave floor was scattered with bones, remnants of past meals. Bone, stone, and ivory shavings and splinters marked places where men had sat and made or repaired tools or hunting weapons, and broken toys spoke of children who had once played in the cave.

We ate the steaming seal meat; drank the fat, scalding broth; and glowed with marvelous warmth. Jes made tea, boiled it until it was coffee-black, and we drank it syrupy-thick with sugar. We were safe, warm, full of food, relaxed and utterly content. Long, long ago, said Jes, Tunit had lived in this cave, a giant people but stupid, and the Inuit had killed them. His stories — part myths, part ancient oral history — spanned the ages. The Primus hissed, and outside roared the storm.

We spread our furs on the ancient sleeping platforms and, minutes later, his deep, even breathing told me that Jes was sound asleep. Cozy in my furry cocoon, I looked at the soot patterns on the cave wall, listened to the eldritch screeching of the storm, and thought sleepily about my other life: our pleasant, book-filled home in Montreal; my wife; our children. It was early May. Maud would be working in the garden. The boys should be home from school. The first tulips would be blooming. As I drifted off to sleep, it seemed part of a dream.

I had been fortunate as a child; I knew exactly what I wanted to be when I grew up: a *Naturforscher*, a biologist-naturalist. In summer in the country, I mothered with great patience and fair success an assortment of wildlife: starlings, a brood of corncrakes, an incredibly demanding and voracious cuckoo. In winter I spent enthralled Sundays at the Natural History Museum in my hometown, Riga, in Latvia. My heroes were the biologists Brehm and Heinroth, Konrad Lorenz, and Jakob von Uexküll, a Baltic German like myself.

The war ended that dream, as it ended so much else. Instead of university, there were years in the Gulag, a brief time in high school in Germany, emigration to Canada, and a job deep in a gold mine in Kirkland Lake in northern Ontario. I was a conscientious but unenthusiastic miner (a shift boss once described me as "a minor miner"), but I did acquire considerable strength and stamina and some very basic English.

I liked northern Ontario — the endless forests, the lonely lakes, the beaver ponds, the wilderness — and my fantasies lured me farther north. While other miners went south for their holidays, I went north, by train to Moosonee and then on Catholic mission boats to the then still extremely isolated Indian villages on James

Bay. One evening we stopped at Cape Hope Island, where Canada's southernmost Inuit lived, and there I met George Wetaltuk.

Wetaltuk was then (in 1952) officially seventy-nine years old. In fact he must have been much older, for he was chief pilot of the Hudson's Bay Company in the nineteenth century and had guided the great sailing ships from England to Charlton Island, which, with its huge warehouses, was then the center of commerce for James Bay. He was a native of the Belcher Islands in Hudson Bay. When Robert J. Flaherty (who much later made the famous film *Nanook of the North*) undertook his first expedition into James Bay and Hudson Bay in 1910 at the request of Canada's railway magnate Sir William Mackenzie, he met Wetaltuk, then already known as "Old Man Wetaltuk," on Charlton Island. Wetaltuk had not been to the virtually totally unknown (by whites) Belcher Islands for more than twenty years, but he drew, with near-total recall, a map for Flaherty of the exceedingly convoluted complex of islands. Flaherty based his expedition on this map, publishing it with his expedition report in the 1918 *American Geographical Review* and noting: "How remarkably accurate this map is!" Wetaltuk had not omitted a single bay or bight and had given the length of the islands to an exactness of 8 miles (12.8 km).

When the railway reached Moosonee in 1933, all freight came in by rail and Charlton Island was abandoned. George Wetaltuk moved to Cape Hope Island to start a new career: he designed and built ships. He had no plan, he used no blueprint; it was all in his head. He worked slowly, meticulously, with a few simple tools, and the ships were perfect, sturdy and capacious and ideal for coastal trading, and they served for years in James Bay, Hudson Bay, and on the Labrador coast. And, in between, he carved magnificent bishops' chairs for several Anglican churches.

Once during these years a plane was forced down near Cape Hope, and Wetaltuk was host to the crew. He asked the pilot why "the thing that flies" did not fly anymore and if he could be shown

At camp, older children often take care of younger siblings.

Expertly wielding a long, sharp knife, a girl at a hunting camp on Baffin Island eats caribou meat while her mother scrapes caribou sinew, which will be made into thread.

Elizabeth Arnajarnek carries her baby in the back pouch of her caribou-skin amautik *in the summer of 1966.*

the broken part. While the crew slept, Wetaltuk was busy all night, filing and hammering away. The next morning he presented the utterly amazed pilot with the spare part he had made during the night. Like the Inuit of the past who were the most self-reliant of people, Wetaltuk had total faith in his ability to create, the same ability and faith that, much later, would enable so many Inuit to change from hunters into world-famous carvers and artists.

This was the man in whose kitchen I and a priest from the mission now sat and drank the usual large mugs of sweet tea. He was obviously very old; his face was dark and deeply lined, the unruly shock of hair nearly white. But his movements were quick, his eyes amused; a proud, independent man, one felt, who had enjoyed life, a man who liked to laugh. He told me tales of long ago, which the priest patiently translated, of hunting polar bears with spears, of kayaking to remote islands to hunt walruses, of meeting the whaling ships that came from Scotland.

At last, late in the night, we left. Wetaltuk took my hand and spoke very solemnly to me, and yet there was a wicked gleam in his

An Inuk boy from Baffin Island.

eyes. I asked the missionary what he had said and, very ill at ease (as Wetaltuk knew he would be), he reluctantly translated an ancient shamanistic benediction whose essence was "may your life be rich with seals." It is an odd coincidence (or is it?) that, much later, I would join scientists who studied arctic seals; become fascinated by seals and their ways; study seals in the Arctic and Antarctic, in southern Africa, Siberia, and South America; and write several books and endless articles about seals. Whenever I do anything with seals, fortune seems to favor me.

From mining I changed to writing and photography, worked for the newspaper in Kirkland Lake, and then, for a while, on Fleet Street in London. From there I moved to Paris and wrote animal stories in execrable French, which kindly editors polished into publishable prose for the magazine *La Vie des Bêtes*. When funds permitted, I traveled: to Africa and the Middle East, but most often to the North. I spent a summer on Spitsbergen with a Scottish expedition, and nearly a year with the Lapps (or Saami, as they prefer to be called), living in their tents, sharing their migrations,

A Polar Inuk returns from hunting at the floe edge.

realizing with sadness that much of their ancient reindeer-herding culture was being lost. (One-quarter of all the words in the Lapp language then pertained to reindeer and reindeer herding; they had, for instance, sixty specific words for every age phase of the reindeer.) Modern mores and southern values were quickly supplanting ancient knowledge and tradition. I liked their life, the freedom of the infinite fjelds, and yet there was a pervasive sadness there, for soon, I felt, this ancient, nature-linked way of life would cease to be.

I married, returned to Canada, tried unsuccessfully to learn to love a nine-to-five job, and started again to write and travel. A magazine sent me north to "do a story on Eskimos." And again I found an ancient culture in disarray and on the verge of vanishing. Change had recently come to the North with devastating speed and abruptness.

The Inuit and their forebears lived in the harshest, most hostile, and potentially most lethal environment ever inhabited by humans. To survive and even thrive in this deadly climate, they invented, in the words of the explorer Vilhjalmur Stefansson, "a system of living perfectly adapted to a cold climate." It took millennia to evolve and perfect this cold-adapted culture.

Change came with glacial slowness: there were inventions, innovations, adaptations, but essentially there was a reassuringly smooth flow of life from generation to generation through the ages. Ancient patterns persisted, old beliefs were repeated, the knowledge and experience acquired over centuries were passed on with great fidelity. The pre-European Inuk, according to the late Diamond Jenness, an anthropologist who had lived for many months early in this century with Inuit who had just been "discovered," was, "to a degree that we today can hardly comprehend... free and independent, master of his own fate... [The Inuit then] were healthy... cheerful and relatively contented — far more contented, I believe, than their

An Inuk schoolboy in Resolute, Canada, in 1967.

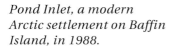

Pond Inlet, a modern Arctic settlement on Baffin Island, in 1988.

present-day descendants, or their white fellow countrymen whose restless civilisation, with its melange of virtues and vices, they are slowly learning to assimilate."

This is, perhaps, too rosy a view of early Inuit life. It was hard, precarious, and in some regions haunted by recurring famines. But it did have that saving grace of contentment known only when a people are secure within their society and in harmony with their natural environment.

That ancient balance was broken when Europeans came to the Arctic — the whalers who took from the North much of its wildlife, the basis of the Inuit's existence, and who brought to the North diseases to which the long-isolated Natives had no immunity. Between 1850 and 1885, the Inuit population of coastal arctic Alaska declined by 50 percent. In two generations, the Mackenzie Delta Inuit were reduced from about 1,000, to fewer than 100. Labrador's Inuit numbered about 3,000 in 1750. In 1946, 750 were left.

With the whales nearly exterminated, the whalers departed, leaving a people wracked by disease and accustomed to, and dependent upon, many southern goods. Into the vacuum created by the whalers' departure stepped the fur traders, and to pay for the southern goods they had come to regard as essential, the Inuit became trappers. Where once they had been poor but independent, they were now dependent and still poor, their ancient autarky destroyed beyond redemption.

In the late 1950s, during the Cold War, a great number of DEW (Distant Early Warning) Line radar stations were built in the Far North. Many Inuit were employed in their construction, and afterward quite a few settled in tents and shacks near these stations, living on income from odd jobs and on handouts. Belatedly, the Canadian government realized it had an "Eskimo problem" on its hands.

In resolving this northern problem, the southern government

Inuit soapstone carvers have become famous for their art.

Octave Sivanertok and his wife stretch a wolf pelt onto a drying board in the kitchen of their home in Repulse Bay, Canada.

Samson Koeenagnak teaches his son how to spot caribou with a telescope on the Barren Grounds in the summer of 1966.

bureaucracy, full of good intentions but essentially paternalistic, adopted a "We must think for them and do what is best for them" philosophy. The people most directly concerned, the Natives of the North, were rarely consulted.

The basic idea was quick assimilation. A government report suggested that "the best way to handle the… [Native] problem was to maintain the adults on relief and separate their children in the school hostels… The young generation would thus fare well in the future, since they would have learned from the school behaviour and attitudes more appropriate to town life, without the disruptive influence of their parents." Inuit children were often punished if they spoke their own language in school, and many did not see their parents for nine months of each year.

The result was a lost generation, neither white nor Inuit, alienated from their parents and their past, their culture, and their land. Many sought solace in alcohol, and thus the North's "terrible liquor problem," as former Northwest Territories commissioner Stuart Hodgson called it, was born.

This, then, was the situation when, more than thirty years ago, a

Moist snow sticks to the sled dogs' paws in the spring. To prevent this, Akeeagok , from Grise Fiord, Ellesmere Island, clips the hairs on a dog's paws in 1967.

magazine sent me north to Frobisher Bay (now Iqaluit) on Baffin Island to write an article about the Inuit. I remembered George Wetaltuk, whose pride and presence had left a lasting impression. Instead, I met a people traumatized by transition, suspended between two worlds — one dear but dying, the other new and alluring but essentially alien.

This was the new "town life" with its problems and its promises, but "on the land," I was told, things were different. There were still camps far from towns and villages where a modified form of traditional life persisted and old customs were cherished, where Inuit were still themselves, their ancient hunting culture still intact, the great skills that had made life possible in the Arctic not yet forgotten.

This, I felt, should somehow be preserved, and when I returned south I went to the government in Ottawa, the fount of power, policy, and funds, and suggested that it might be a good idea to record as much as possible of this rapidly vanishing Inuit culture, that I would like to do it, and would they help me? The bureaucrats listened politely and then explained to me a few facts of life. To begin with, Natives did not have cultures, they merely had life-styles totally unsuited to our era, to the "new North," and the sooner they became like us, the better. And if the Natives were going to be studied, it was going to be done by competent, government-approved scientists. It was clear that the bureaucrats in their neat offices felt there was something not at all *comme il faut* about this idea of "going to live with the Natives." They did nothing to actually hinder me, but they certainly were not going to help.

So I did it alone: first short trips of a few weeks, then longer ones to more remote camps, and soon I spent six months of every year in the Arctic, commuting between two worlds: the slowly vanishing world of the traditional Arctic hunter, and my home and family in Montreal.

Each region of the North had special traditions, its own history. Ancient tools survived here and there: the people of Repulse Bay still use the leister, the traditional, trident-like fishing spear; the Polar Inuit of northwest Greenland hunt seals and whales with the spear-thrower, an invention that goes back tens of thousands of years to Upper Paleolithic times; some people on Little Diomede Island in Bering Strait use the ancient bow drill; and a few Siberian Inuit still know how to use bolas. Each trip brought new knowledge, new friends, a better appreciation of the ancient art of Arctic living.

The Inuit, over a period of thirty years, from Greenland across Canada's North to Alaska and Siberia, put me up and put up with me, for weeks and often for months. I shared their food, their homes, their travels, their hardships, their happiness. They were sometimes exasperated (after all, it must be a nuisance to have an inquisitive stranger in your bedroom for months and months and months), but generally they showed great forbearance and tolerance, and were pleased that I wanted to learn and write about "the old way of life."

And so I came to sleep in that bone-strewn cave on the northwest coast of Greenland, wrapped in furs, next to Jes Qujaukitsoq, warm and content, safe from the raging fury of the storm. The storm lasted two days. We ate lots of seal meat and drank pots of tea, and Jes told me stories from times long past in the gray light of the cave.

As so often in the Arctic after an evil storm, the weather became sublime: the air as cool and clear as chilled champagne, the sky deep blue, the snow and ice aglitter. Our dogs emerged from their snow beds, shook themselves, and yipped and howled, eager to go. We loaded the sled and headed home for Qaanaaq, the main settlement of the Polar Inuit, the northernmost people in the world. The long sled slid smoothly over the wind-packed snow, the huskies trotted happily, and life was very good. I thought again of an ancient Inuit poem that I love:

> *And yet, there is only*
> *One great thing,*
> *The only thing:*
> *To live;*
> *To see in huts and on journeys*
> *The great day that dawns,*
> *And the light that fills the world.*

CHAPTER ONE

THEY CAME OUT OF ASIA

*[In the beginning] the world was
emptiness. Then two men grew up
from a hummock of earth. They were
born and full grown all at once.
And they wished to have children.
A magic song changed one of them
into a woman, and they had children.
These were our earliest forefathers,
and from them all the lands
were peopled.*

— Inuit creation legend
told by Tuglik of the Igloolik area in 1922

I LIVED FOR FIVE MONTHS ON LITTLE DIOMEDE ISLAND IN
Bering Strait — three months in 1975 and two months fifteen
years later, in 1990. The island, which belongs to Alaska, is 2.5
miles (4 km) long and 1.5 miles (2.4 km) wide and rises steeply on
all sides to its 1,309-foot (399-m) summit. Only at its northwest
corner is the slope gentler, and that's where the Inuit village of
Ignaluk is tacked against the mountainside. It is a small village
(population 171 in 1990), but it has been continuously inhabited
for well over 2,000 years. It is older than Paris, London, or Berlin.

Occasionally, in 1975, a helicopter rose from Big Diomede
Island, 3 miles (4.8 km) away and Soviet-owned, and flew east.
After 1.5 miles (2.4 km), it halted abruptly, as if it had hit a glass
wall, then flew north or south along this line and returned.

That borderline, precisely in the middle between the two islands,
divides two worlds: Asia and America, the United States and
Russia; it then (in 1975) separated two of the world's great
ideologies, communism and capitalism. It even separates today and
tomorrow, for here the border coincides with the international
dateline. Later, when we passed this line on our hunting trips, we
moved from one day to the next, and coming home, as it says in a
limerick, "we returned on the previous day."

What is now a border and a barrier was once a bridge, the Bering
Land Bridge, or Beringia, a vast and vanished land. During the ice
ages of the Pleistocene, immense mile-thick ice sheets covered
about 6 million square miles (15.5 million km²) of North America

*A visitor stands on an
erratic on the northwest
coast of Greenland.
According to Inuit legend,
the last Tunerq (Dorset-
culture Inuk) was shot
upon this large boulder.*

The great musk-ox was probably the main prey of the earliest High Arctic hunters.

and a large part of Eurasia; 8 million cubic miles (10.7 billion m^3) of water were locked within this monstrous mass of ice. The level of the world's oceans was nearly 400 feet (122 m) lower than it is now, and a 1,000-mile (1600-km)-wide land corridor connected Asia and America. Across it from Asia came many of today's North American mammals, among them the moose, the musk-ox, and the caribou. Moving in the other direction were the ancestors of the Eurasian horse and the camel.

Among the last to cross the great tundra plains of Beringia from Asia into the great, game-rich continent of America, perhaps past the craggy mountains whose tops today stick out of the sea as the Diomede Islands, were the ancestors of the Indians and the Inuit.

The Inuit's forebears, paleoanthropologists believe, were a people of Arctic Mongoloid stock; their legacy is the bluish Mongolian spot at the base of the spine, which every Inuit baby has at birth. They crossed Bering Strait about 8,000 years ago. The Indians' ancestors had already pre-empted most of the Americas, but the Arctic was empty.

For a hunting people, the Arctic had its attractions: millions of caribou, tens of thousands of musk-oxen, millions of birds and seals, and immense pods of whales and walruses. Yet the first Arctic people seem to have been poorly prepared to harvest this wealth, and they must have led lives of incredible hardship.

The people of the Arctic Small Tool Tradition — so called for their distinctively minute blades and spear points, chipped with consummate craftmanship from chert, flint, and quartz — spread eastward from Alaska about 5,000 years ago, and within the span of roughly a thousand years occupied the Arctic all the way north to

Ellesmere Island and east to East Greenland.

Today, on Ellesmere Island and northern Greenland, regions they seem to have favored (perhaps because musk-oxen, common in this area, were their main prey), the mean January temperature is –30°F (–34°C), temperatures can drop to –70°F (–57°C), winter storms are frequent, and the sun sets on October 20 and does not rise above the horizon again until early March. In the Thule region of northwest Greenland, now home of the Polar Inuit, only one month, July, has an average temperature above the freezing point.

Yet these first people of the Arctic lacked the toggle harpoon so essential for successful sea-mammal hunting. They had neither boats nor dog teams. Worst of all, they did not have oil lamps, only small open stone hearths in which they burned rare twigs of dwarf willow, dried moss, and the bones of the animals they killed. They lived year-round in small unheated tents, and from late October until early March in perpetual darkness.

Cold inhibits both growth and decay. In the Qaanaaq region of Greenland, for instance, the growing season is about three weeks of the year. Plant growth, therefore, is exceedingly slow. Some arctic lichens grow at an average rate of about 1.5 inches (4 cm) in diameter every thousand years. Decay (think of the steak in your freezer or mammoths that can be eaten after 40,000 years of having been sealed in permafrost) is equally slow, because of the cold, fewer bacteria, and, usually, a very dry climate.

In the High Arctic, human disturbance is so rare, decay so slow, that not much changes through the ages. Several times on my long walks on northern Ellesmere Island I found camps of the first Arctic people. They looked as if the families had left a few months

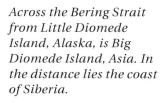

Across the Bering Strait from Little Diomede Island, Alaska, is Big Diomede Island, Asia. In the distance lies the coast of Siberia.

ago: the central hearth of flat stones, a few still fire-blackened, the circle of stones that once held down the edges of the tent. But 4,000 years had passed since people lived here under these harsh conditions; it seems a miracle of the human spirit that they survived. But survive they did, and they had children who must have laughed and played around this camp, as Inuit children still laugh and play far into the luminous Arctic night at summer camps today. And these ancient people of the Arctic who lived at the very edge of possible life, created not quick, rough, utilitarian tools, but tiny masterpieces, with an evident love for the material (they preferred glass-clear or tinted flints and quartzes) and a superb feeling for form and design.

From these people of the Arctic Small Tool Tradition other cultures evolved, the pre-Dorset and, about 800 B.C., the Dorset culture, which spread from its core area in northern Hudson Bay across most of the North American Arctic. Their culture was distinctly Eskimoan. They had more elaborate tools and hunting implements and a way of life much better suited to far-northern living than had their predecessors. And they held sway over the Arctic for nearly 2,000 years.

They vanished 800 years ago, vanquished or absorbed by newcomers, people of the Thule culture, but today's Inuit still

These Dorset-culture petroglyphs were carved into this soapstone on Qikertaaluk Island, Hudson Strait, perhaps a thousand years ago.

The igloo, once the winter home of many Inuit, is now built by hunters as a shelter for the night on long trips.

remember the Dorset-culture people. They call them Tunit, a race of moody giants, preternaturally powerful, irascible but stupid and, compared to the Inuit, still poorly equipped. They did not have dog teams, say the Inuit, but pulled small, ivory-shod sleds themselves, and they did not know how to make waterproof sealskin boots. But they were so powerful, Igloolik Inuit say, "they could haul a [1-ton/0.9-tonne] walrus home as easily as we pull a little seal." When the Danish ethnologist Knud Rasmussen crossed Rae Isthmus near northernmost Hudson Bay in the early 1920s, he came upon "three tent rings made of gigantic stones," and the Inuit told him they were made "by the first people that lived in the country, the Tunit."

The oral history of the Inuit is marvelously vivid. While I lived with the Polar Inuit of northwest Greenland, I often traveled to the floe edge with an older hunter, Masautsiaq Eipe and his beautiful, vivacious wife, Sofie Arnapalâq, the sister of Jes Qujaukitsoq with whom I camped in the cave. (In the past each Inuk had his or her own name and kept that name throughout life.) One day we stopped at Natsiliviq, a broad peninsula with many semisubterranean stone houses, some very old, some inhabited by Inuit until just a generation ago. Sofie, who loved to gossip, told me slightly ribald stories about the people who had lived there (in other lands she would have made an excellent society columnist).

Masautsiaq listened with tolerant amusement and then told me in meticulous detail the ancient history of the place. "Long, long

The walls of this Thule-culture house in Canada's Arctic are made of twelve whale skulls.

ago," he said, "Inuit and Tunit lived together in this land. But the Tunit were dangerous; they liked to wrestle and play games, and they were so strong, they killed people. Then the Inuit shot them with arrows, and finally only a few Tunit were left and they lived here at Natsiliviq. You see that big stone" — he pointed at an enormous erratic near the shore, surrounded by a layer of seal and walrus bones — "the last Tunerq climbed that rock and the Inuit shot arrows into him and he fell down dead. And he was the last of all the Tunit."

Something like that probably happened 800 years ago, for stories from the past, I learned, were transmitted with utmost fidelity from generation to generation. In 1968, Tomassi Mangiuk of Ivujivik, an Inuit village on the northwest tip of arctic Quebec, was telling me tales of *taipsomani*, the past of his people, of trips to the nearby Digges Islands with their immense colony of thick-billed murres, and how they hunted the birds and collected eggs from narrow ledges of the 1,000- foot (300-m)-high cliffs.

"Once an *umiaraaluk* [great boat] came, and white men rowed ashore. They made signs that they were hungry. They wanted meat. They gave the people knives. There was a fight. One Inuk was killed. And the Inuit killed some white men. The others fled back to their big boat, there was a noise like thunder and one kayak was destroyed…" I suddenly realized with a jolt that the story he was telling me in such graphic detail was of that fateful day, July 29, 1611, when four members of Henry Hudson's mutinous crew were killed by the Inuit. One member of that ill-starred expedition, Abacuk Pricket, kept a written record, and it tallies in every detail

This ancient and ingenious beehive-shaped stone trap on Ellesmere Island was used by Inuit to capture arctic foxes.

with the story memorized by the Inuit and told to me by Tomassi Mangiuk 350 years later.

The Inuit's cold-adapted culture did not reach a state of near-perfection until the arrival of the Thule-culture people, who moved eastward from Alaska about A.D. 800, and within less than 200 years spread across most of the North American Arctic, displacing or absorbing the Dorset people.

Superb sea-mammal hunters, Thule-culture Inuit pursued and

killed everything, from the small ringed seal to the giant bowhead whale, and, according to archaeologist Robert McGhee of the Canadian Museum of Civilization, they had evolved "a technology more complex than that of any other preindustrial society, which allowed not only an economically efficient but also comfortable way of life throughout arctic North America."

The Thule Inuit invented, perfected, and passed on to Inuit of historic times such a plethora of specialized tools and hunting equipment that the late James A. Ford of the American Museum of Natural History described them as "gadget burdened."

The tool kit, for instance, used by Inuit not long ago to hunt seals at their *agloos*, the snow-covered breathing holes through the ice, consisted of about forty items, from the thin, slightly curved bone probe to determine the shape of the agloo, to *tutereark*, the piece of thick caribou winter fur on which the hunter stood so that no sound would warn the seal of his presence.

The Inuit achieved this broad-ranging yet highly specialized Arctic material culture against what seem insuperable odds. Not only was their land exceedingly cold, hostile, and barren, it was also poor in those raw materials most societies have found essential. Metal was rare: meteoric iron, brittle and hard to work, was found in the Cape York region of northwest Greenland, and native copper in a few areas of the central Canadian Arctic. Driftwood was abundant along Alaska's coast and east past the Mackenzie River delta; it was rare in the eastern Arctic and virtually nonexistent in the central Arctic. That left stone, ice, snow, and sod as the most readily available and most widely used materials that the land and the sea provided. Infinitely more important were the materials they obtained from the animals they killed: bone, horn, baleen, antlers, teeth, ivory, furs, skins, sinews, and intestinal tissues.

As Dionyse Settle, the Elizabethan chronicler of explorer Martin Frobisher's second expedition to Baffin Island, so shrewdly observed in 1577: "Those beastes, flesh, fishes, and fowles, which they kil, they are meate, drinke, apparel, houses, bedding, hose, shooes, thred, saile for their boates… and almost all their riches."

In the thirteenth century, the climate began to change. It became much colder; it was the beginning of the so-called Little Ice Age that lasted until the 1850s. Frost killed the orange trees of northern China, and England's vineyards. The Dutch skated on frozen canals; the English roasted oxen on the frozen Thames; and in far-off Greenland the Vikings died out, victims of cold, isolation, and disease.

In the Arctic, the winter ice became thicker and lasted longer. Bowhead whales and perhaps walruses, the "bulk-food" prey of the Thule-culture hunters, may have left the northernmost seas, and the Inuit abandoned the High Arctic regions (only one group, the Polar Inuit, remained, about 200 people living in total isolation

In a few regions of the Arctic, the Inuit found native copper and made the blades for knives from it; the handles were made of bone.

from the rest of humanity for many centuries). The people dispersed, becoming more migratory, and the modern phase of Inuit life began, tiny pockets of people scattered across the immensity of the Arctic.

They had no contact with other people, except on rare and then often fatal occasions with Indians, whom they both feared and despised, until the fateful arrival of the Europeans. First came the explorers, aliens from an alien world, who found the Inuit as fascinating and odd as the Inuit found them; but their impact on the Inuit's hunting culture was minimal.

Then came the whalers, the fur traders, the missionaries, the Mounties (Royal Canadian Mounted Police), and suddenly, starting in the 1950s, change came in big leaps: schools were built, camps closed, towns grew up, a steady stream of advisers and educators arrived in the North, and the Inuit were yanked *nolens volens* into the mainstream of Canadian society.

Change was near-total, the old ways doomed. The Inuit tried to cope with big problems — how to create an acceptable amalgam of past and present — and with tiny problems that were merely vexing, like the white man's endless curiosity. Ekalun of Bathurst Inlet, with whom I lived for six months, was about ten years old when he and his people were "discovered" by members of the 1913–18 Stefansson–Anderson expedition. "What were they like?" I asked. "Just like you, Kabloo," Ekalun shot back. "Forever asking questions."

THE LOST TRIBE

In 1967, I lived some months at Coral Harbour on Southampton Island in northern Hudson Bay and often traveled with Tommy Nakoolak, then, at sixty-two, patriarch of the island's sizable Nakoolak clan. Of Knud Rasmussen, the great Danish ethnologist, it was said that he was the only man known who collected old women. They, of course, were the repositories of the ancient tales he loved and recorded. Similarly, whenever possible, I lived and traveled with older Inuit who told and taught me many things — the lore, the legends, the skills of their people.

Tommy Nakoolak was small and wiry, kind and considerate, and he owned a Peterhead boat, the *Tereglu* (the word for a baby bearded seal), which he handled as if it were a racing yawl. One day along Coats Island, south of Southampton Island, he spotted a herd of walruses on a rocky promontory. "You want pictures?" he asked, and when I said yes, he swung the boat around and headed full speed for the rocks. He sheered past them so closely, I tensed instinctively for the coming crash, but Tommy only smiled. Like many old-time Inuit, he had an astounding geographical memory and knew every rock and ridge along hundreds of miles of coast.

One day, while his sons were hunting caribou on Coats Island, Tommy said: "Come, I'll show you something." He took the *Tereglu* to a secluded bay near Cape Pembroke. Ashore were ancient stone houses, man-high cairns, box-like graves built of large flat stones, and everywhere masses of bleached bones of caribou, walrus, bowhead whale, and seal. "This is where the Sadlermiut lived," said Tommy. A mysterious, long-isolated Stone Age people, the Sadlermiut were briefly known to the outside world and then all were killed by a whaler-brought disease in the winter of 1902. They may even have been Tunit, the powerful Dorset-culture people. Extinct everywhere else for 800 years, they had found a final refuge on these isolated islands. (The people who now live on Southampton Island are descendants of mainland Inuit brought by whalers and traders to the island to replace the extinct Sadlermiut.)

The Sadlermiut were "discovered" in the summer of 1824 by the explorer Captain G.F. Lyon of the Royal Navy. He anchored his ship, HMS *Griper*, off Cape Pembroke. From the camp which Tommy Nakoolak was showing me, a man approached the *Griper*, riding on a most peculiar craft. It consisted of "three inflated seal-skins, connected most ingeniously by blown intestines, so that his vessel was extremely buoyant." The man's legs dangled in the water while he propelled this strange float toward the ship with a narrow-bladed paddle made of whale bone. The poor man had never seen other humans before and he was afraid: "his teeth chattered and himself and seal-skins trembled in unison."

Lyon went ashore. The people were shy but friendly, of "mild manners, quiet speech, and as grateful for kindness, as they were anxious to return it." The men wore pants of polar-bear fur; their mittens were the skins of murres, feathers inside. The women were slightly tattooed, and "their hair was twisted into a short club, which hung over each temple." The men's topknots were even more impressive: "Each man had an immense mass of hair as large as the head of a child, rolled into the form of a ball, and projecting from the rise of the forehead."

Once the Sadlermiut had been numerous. At Native Point on Southampton Island, the archaeologist Henry B. Collins of the Smithsonian Institution found, in 1954, "the largest aggregation of old Eskimo house ruins in the Canadian Arctic." But whalers began to stop at the islands and contact with another world was fatal to the long-isolated people. When the whaling captain George Comer visited Southampton Island in 1896, only seventy Sadlermiut were left. Comer admired the strength and courage of these "fearless people" who had only stone-tipped harpoons and spears: "For an Eskimo in his frail kayak to attempt to capture a [50-ton/45-tonne] whale with the primitive implements which they manufactured meant great courage."

In the fall of 1902, the whaler *Active* stopped at Southampton

On Coats Island in Hudson Bay, once home of the now extinct Sadlermiut, the remnants of an ancient house are surrounded by the animal bones of long-ago feasts.

Island. One sailor was sick; he may have had typhus or typhoid. Sadlermiut visited the ship and took the disease back to their village. That winter the last Sadlermiut died in lonely agony upon their island. Collins studied their house ruins and graves in 1954 and 1955 and "found evidence that the Sadlermiut descended from the Dorsets — that they were in fact the last survivors of the Dorset culture."

CHAPTER TWO

THE NORTHERNMOST PEOPLE

ONCE, A THOUSAND YEARS AGO AND EARLIER, INUIT OF VARIOUS cultures and traditions inhabited the Arctic as far north as there is land. But when the climate deteriorated during the Little Ice Age that lasted roughly from the thirteenth century until the 1850s, and whales and walruses abandoned the ice-choked far-northern seas, people left the High Arctic islands and northernmost Greenland, or died out.

Only one group remained; in total isolation, the Polar Inuit of northwest Greenland inhabited a region that was exceptionally rich in game, a hunter's arctic Eden. As time passed, the memory of other people faded; they became part of mythology: "Once upon a time other humans existed…." But now they, the 200-odd Polar Inuit, were the only people on earth, living in a land bounded by ice: Ellesmere Island's glacier-capped coast to the west; the mighty Humboldt Glacier to the north; to the south the immense glaciers that flow into Melville Bay; and to the east, beyond the narrow ice-free coastal strip of land they inhabited, Sermerssuaq, the "giant glacier," the 2-mile (3.2-km)-thick ice cap of Greenland.

With the end of the Napoleonic wars, the British Navy had ships and men to spare and, prodded by Sir Joseph Banks, president of the prestigious Royal Society, decided to resume the quest for that Holy Grail of Arctic exploration — the Northwest Passage. In the spring of 1818, Captain John Ross sailed for Greenland with the sloop *Isabella* and the brig *Alexander*, accompanied by the artist John Sacheuse, a native of Greenland and fluent in several Greenland dialects as well as in English. Ross rammed his ships through the pack ice. On August 8, 1818, in northern Melville Bay, he saw men on the ice. The Polar Inuit had been discovered.

To lure them closer, Ross ordered presents put on the ice. (He had come well prepared: his supply of gifts for the Natives of the High Arctic included 15 pounds [6.75 kg] of vermilion paint, 102 pounds [46 kg] of snuff, 13 cases of cowrie shells, and 40 umbrellas.) Ross and his officers — in full-dress naval uniforms, with cocked hats, ceremonial swords, and gold-glittering epaulettes — walked across the ice to meet the fur-clad Natives. They

Equipped with guns, harpoons, and lances, two Polar Inuit walk from their camp to the floe edge to hunt seals and whales in the spring of 1971.

expressed "extreme terror and amazement," Ross observed. "Do you come from the moon?" they asked.

They thought the ships were giant birds. "We have seen them move their wings [sails]," they told Sacheuse. He persuaded a few to come aboard ship, and "their astonishment was unbounded." Here there was mystery and wealth beyond the wildest dreams of mortals, and they reacted to it with a touching mixture of awe and avarice. They marveled at glass as "ice" that does not melt, but any food offered them, such as biscuits or salt meat, "they spat out in disgust." Metal and wood were precious, more precious than gold is to us, and for them the ships were crammed with treasures. Occasionally, greed exceeded discretion. One man tried to abscond with a spare mast; another had a crack at hauling away the armorer's huge anvil.

After Ross came the whalers, with such regularity the Polar Inuit called them *upernagdlit*, the bringers of spring. As elsewhere in the Arctic, they also brought more deadly gifts, diseases to which the long-isolated people had no resistance. By 1861, only a hundred Polar Inuit were left.

They increased slowly, helped Robert Peary to reach the North Pole (which they derisively call Kingmersoriartorfigssuak, the place where one only eats dogs), and became close friends with Knud Rasmussen and Peter Freuchen, who settled with them early this century, opened a store, and with a fine flair for the dramatic called the place Thule, the ancient Greco-Roman name for the utmost bound of the habitable world. The Polar Inuit, Rasmussen, and Freuchen were of a fiber. "Give me winter, give me dogs, and you can keep the rest," Rasmussen wrote.

In 1951, the Polar Inuit, then numbering 300, were still very isolated, their only brief contact with the outside world the visit of

Sofie Eipe.

Masautsiaq Eipe.

the annual supply ship. That summer the Americans came to build the giant Thule Air Base. An armada of ships arrived, and thousands (at one time, more than 10,000) servicemen. Some Polar Inuit who had gone north in spring to hunt found, upon their return in late fall, a full-grown military town on the broad, flat peninsula they used to call Pitufiq, the place where one leaves boats.

To the Polar Inuit it was part miracle, part nightmare. "Ships came and planes and more planes. And people. So many people. We had never seen so many people. They wanted to buy everything: our clothes, our tools, walrus tusks, narwhal tusks, kayak models. And all the things that were of great value to us meant nothing to them." Sofie Arnapalâq recalled the invasion of their isolated world twenty years earlier as we sat on the long, fur-covered dog-team sled at the floe edge, waiting for seal and hoping for narwhal. They had lived for a year near the noisy air base. Then the Polar Inuit moved farther north, to the village of Qaanaaq, which is where I met Sofie and Masautsiaq Eipe.

Our acquaintance began with a bad *faux pas*. I had met them only briefly, a beautiful young woman and an elderly man, and had assumed they were father and daughter. They said I could come with them to the floe edge. The next day on the sledge, I asked about her father. Sofie stared at me: "You mean Masautsiaq? He's not my father. He's my husband!" Masautsiaq laughed good-naturedly, and Sofie, fifty-four years old and eleven times a grandmother, was absolutely delighted.

Sofie had raven-black hair, a fine figure, and smooth skin. She dressed with exquisite care in the finest furs, as befitted the wife of a great hunter. She wore a fox-fur parka, warm and elegant, with a high, helmet-like hood; pert little fox-fur pants; hip-high, pure-white sealskin boots fringed at the top with the long silver-glistening mane fur of a polar bear, and inner boots made of down-soft arctic hare fur. A layer of dried grass between outer and inner boot provided near-perfect insulation. Since these high boots bend only slightly at the knee, Sofie had the distinctive, perforce rather stiff-legged walk of Polar Inuit women.

Masautsiaq's clothes were warm and durable: a *kulitaq*, a caribou-skin parka; the distinctive Polar Inuit *nanut*, pants made of polar-bear skin, warm, waterproof and exceedingly strong; outer boots of sealskin and inner boots of hare. "In this well-ventilated costume the man will sleep upon his sledge with the atmosphere at 93° below our freezing point," the explorer Elisha Kent Kane observed more than a century ago.

They still do. I found out the hard way. I was city-soft when I arrived in Qaanaaq and found the April weather cutting cold. Agpalinguaq, a strong, taciturn young hunter, was the first to take me along to the floe edge. His well-fed, well-rested dogs ran fast,

Hidden behind a white shield mounted on a small sled, a hunter creeps toward a sleeping seal in early summer.

Using dog teams, Polar Inuit haul killed walruses onto the ice.

and in eight hours, with a brief stop to make tea, we were at the open water. We sat and waited all night. Seals surfaced in the distance. Agpalinguaq scratched the ice, whistled softly, made the many sounds to which a curious seal might respond and come close. None did. The damp cold seeped through my clothes. I shivered and was hungry.

In the morning, the wind picked up, the sea was rough, seal-hunting impossible. "We sleep," Agpalinguaq said. How about some food first? I asked. "No food," he said. To have taken food along would have been an admission that he lacked faith in his skills as a hunter. The tent? "No tent," he said. We slept on the sled — he soundly, I poorly.

Agpalinguaq finally shot and harpooned a seal early next morning;

it was forty-eight hours since we had eaten. We hauled the seal onto the ice and he slit it open; we drank handfuls of warm blood, then ate the rich raw liver together with snippets of blubber, and vital warmth spread through my body.

We spent a week at the floe edge, Agpalinguaq waiting with the endless patience and concentration of the true hunter. When we returned, his sled was loaded with seals, food for his family and dogs.

Trips with Sofie and Masautsiaq were easier. Sofie liked comfort; we had a roomy tent and always plenty of food. One of their grandsons often traveled with us, and Masautsiaq told him about the land and sea: "There is a current near that coast and the ice is very thin; that valley leads to a lake with many fish; people used to live at that spot, you can still see the house ruins; that slope is a good place to set snares for hares…" Masautsiaq's knowledge was astounding, learned from his father when he was young and added to during a lifetime of keen observation and travel, and now he was passing the knowledge on to his grandson. Later, I asked the boy what he planned to be when he grew up. "A mechanic," he said.

It was May now, and often sunny and warm. Many hunters came from Qaanaaq. Some brought their families, and the children played far into the luminous night. The hunters stood at the ice edge in easy viewing distance of one another. If one got a narwhal, all rushed to his assistance and were then entitled to a share of the kill, the portions established by age-old custom.

One morning Masautsiaq woke up, smiled happily, and said: "Today I get a narwhal!" He had dreamed of narwhal, and Polar Inuit regard dreams as omens. He waited, patiently, observant as always; he shot and harpooned two seals, but we saw no whales. Gulls squabbled in the distance. We took sled and dogs to have a look. In the deep, Greenland sharks were tearing a dead narwhal to pieces, perhaps one killed days ago by a hunter's bullet. Bits of blubber drifted to the surface, and also a good-sized piece of *muktuk*, narwhal skin. We hooked it, hauled it onto the ice, trimmed

Children romp near the floe edge.

Sofie, Masautsiaq, and me near the floe edge in the spring of 1971.

it a bit and ate it: it is crunchy, has a delicious fresh-hazelnut flavor, and is extremely rich in vitamin C. "That was the narwhal of my dream," Masautsiaq said, with a rueful smile.

Some spring nights at the floe edge were pure magic: the air cold and calm and crystal clear, the water glowing in the sunlit night, the ice softly opalescent, the light honey-yellow on the far mountains. Milky-white beluga whales swam in the distance; we could hear them trill and grunt. Flocks of eider ducks flew low above the water, mirrored in the lambent sea. Ivory gulls, long-winged and pure white, circled above us, their cries strident and tern-like. From here and there across the ice drifted the laughter of playing children.

And then the dovekies came — thousands, tens of thousands, perhaps hundreds of thousands, dark amorphous clouds of birds against the luminous blue-green of the sky, all heading northwest toward the immense breeding slopes of the Siorapaluk-Etah region, flying fast, urgently, to keep their date with destiny.

May, in the Polar Inuit dialect, is called *Apaliarssuit tikiarfiat,* the dovekies return. They are black and white cigar-shaped seabirds, starling-sized, but chubbier. An estimated 80 million breed in the High Arctic, 30 million alone in the region where the Polar Inuit live, and to them they always were, and still are, a vital food.

Seal hunting might fail, walruses might avoid their coasts one year, but the dovekies always came, punctual, predictable, and in millions.

In June, many Qaanaaq hunters sledged north to Siorapaluk, the northernmost village in the world and close to one of the main dovekie slopes. They took me along, and I lived there with Inuterssuaq Uvdloriaq (the brother of Peter Freuchen's wife, Navarana), an old hunter of great skill and dignity, and his wife, Naduq. Their home was small and modest: a one-room structure crowded with hunting weapons, tools, dishes, pots, and books. Inuterssuaq had guided many expeditions; on the wall hung citations and medals he had received from the King of Denmark. He had never gone to school, was entirely self-educated, an avid reader, and also a writer, the historian of his people.

Our days were spent on the 1,000-foot (305-m)-high scree slopes, now speckled with dovekies and with the bright-orange, nitrophilous lichen *Caloplaca elegans,* which the Polar Inuit, less elegantly, call *sunain anak,* the sun's excrement. Naduq, sixty-two years old, not quite 5 feet (150 cm) tall, with a slim, boyish figure and a deeply wrinkled face, clambered with cat-like agility up and down the steep, treacherous rock slope. She carried an *ipu* (a long-handled net), hid behind boulders or low outcroppings of rock — some, to judge by lichen encrustation, very old — and scooped with immense speed and skill the low-flying dovekies out of the air, killing them instantly.

Her sealskin bag full of dovekies, Naduq descends the steep scree slope.

On good days, Naduq and Inuterssuaq caught between 300 and 600 dovekies, and we carried heavy leather bags full of birds down to the sledge and dog team parked at the base of the slope. Most dovekies were cached for the winter, but some we ate immediately. Naduq, amused by my ineptness, showed me how to do it: first, one skins the dovekies and chews the fat off the skin (I ate a lot of feathers until I got the knack of it), and then one eats the lean meat of the bird together with bits of whale or seal blubber. Until one develops the Inuit's speed and dexterity in eating the little birds, a dovekie supper tends to be somewhat like a Roman feast of larks and nightingales, long on show and short on substance.

Naduq knew more than a hundred cat's-cradle figures; she made them with string and incredibly nimble fingers. A few figures, like "copulation," were risqué. The usually grave Inuterssuaq egged her on; Naduq made them, but was embarrassed, like a young girl. In the western Arctic, I told them, Inuit make a figure they call *kalifaiciaq* (it represents the mammoth, and it has always intrigued me that the memory of this long-extinct animal should have survived, perhaps 10,000 years or more, in this Inuit string game). "We know it too," Inuterssuaq said. "But we call it *kilifagssuk*," Naduq informed me as she made the figure. It was identical to the one I had seen made by Copper Inuit, 3,000 miles (4800 km) to the west. "What is a kilifagssuk?" I asked Inuterssuaq. "It means an animal," he explained, "a very big animal. It has four legs. It is like a

musk-ox but much bigger. It existed a long time ago. But no one here has ever seen it. Even the oldest people have never seen it."

It is indicative of the wide distribution of string games that the anthropologist Diamond Jenness, who published in 1924 a monograph on the string figures made by the Copper Inuit, had earlier published a paper on Papuan cat's cradles from New Guinea. In 1913, when Jenness lived among Inuit in northern Alaska, he noted that virtually all adults were adept at making cat's-cradle figures, but by far the most skillful of all was a woman who was blind: "With a single loop of string she could produce an amazing variety of fanciful birds and animals, and people engaged in different pursuits. Some of the figures would dance for her, or race from one hand to the other; and as they ran she chanted different refrains that brought tears of laughter to the eyes of her listeners."

In mid-July, the ice broke up. It was the brief season of open water, when seals and whales were hunted with kayaks. I went to Inerssussat, a famous whale-hunting camp just 2 miles (3.2 km) east of Qaanaaq. Masautsiaq was there, and Sofie, Jes Qujaukitsoq and his family, and many other hunters I knew. The men built kayak skeletons; the women covered them with sewn-together sealskins. The men carved new ivory harpoons, the inset blade a razor-sharp piece of metal, taken from an old saw; the women sewed new boots. We fished for sculpin, big-headed bony little fish. And we waited and watched. Until someone sang out: "*Kilaluga-hoi*! (The narwhals are coming!)" Far down great Inglefield Bay, the sharp-eyed Inuit had spotted the telltale spouts of the whales.

The men paddled their kayaks far out into the bay, then fanned out into the anticipated path of the approaching whales, hiding near ice floes and keeping totally quiet. High on a bluff above the sea, women and children gathered and followed with passionate interest the ancient drama of the hunt. The whales, several scattered pods with a total of more than a hundred animals, swam leisurely up the bay, bound for the food-rich region near great glaciers at the head of the bay where they would spend the summer.

One whale, a large male, swam close by the ice floe that hid Jes's

Masautsiaq walks into a lonely valley, hoping to find arctic hares.

A kayak hunter returns in the golden light of the evening.

kayak. Jes, with a few cautious but powerful paddle strokes, slipped into the wake of the whale. Narwhals are acutely aware of danger from any direction, but not if it is directly behind them. Jes paddled with all his might; on the bluff, the women screamed with excitement. When Jes was close to the whale, he threw his heavy harpoon with one smooth, incredibly powerful motion. It hit, and the whale was doomed. The other kayaks converged at high speed to help in the kill; the sequence of their arrival and help would determine, by ancient custom, their share of the whale.

They tied their kayaks in tandem and hauled the whale toward camp. Jes, the victor, the provider of food, paddled triumphantly in front. But when they hauled the whale ashore, the hordes arrived: every wage-employed man in Qaanaaq and his family came running to claim a share of the whale. Meat from a newly caught animal was traditionally shared. That is Inuit custom. But wages were never shared. That is European custom.

The cultures clashed and slowly the hunters left Inerssussat and settled at camps farther up the bay. There hunter shared with hunter as they had done in the past when, as Elisha Kent Kane observed in the 1850s, the Polar Inuit "exist in love and community of resources as a single family."

A Polar Inuk child plays with the handle of the dog team whip.

THE PERFECT CRAFT

When the Polar Inuit hunted at the floe edge, one couple kept apart. Inuteq was then seventy-five years old; he was a great traveler and owned one of the finest dog teams in the region. I once made a trip with him and we had to round a cape on an ice foot, a slanting, slippery, narrow ledge of ice high above open water. Aleqasinguaq, his wife, went ahead and called the badly frightened dogs, and Inuteq steered and held the heavy sled with power and precision. But his eyesight was failing, and his wife, a crack shot, did most of the hunting for him. This shamed him deeply, and at the floe edge the couple kept their distance.

They camped with us at Inerssussat when we waited in July for the narwhals to come. Inuteq had arrived at camp with two three-quarter-inch (19-mm) planks, and using a knife, saw, and plane transformed them into a beautifully made kayak skeleton. Not a nail or screw was used in the construction. End pieces were doweled; other sections were expertly tied to make the craft both strong and flexible.

While Inuteq cut and carved each piece and then fitted it into the growing kayak skeleton with meticulous precision, Aleqasinguaq scraped, cleaned, and depilated eleven ringed-seal skins and sewed them into a long continuous band.

When the skeleton was ready, she and all the other women in camp covered the kayak. They sewed the wet skins (which would dry, contract, and be drum-tight) onto the boat skeleton with the "lost stitch technique," a double seam in which the needle never pierces the skin. Their thread was made of narwhal sinew; it is

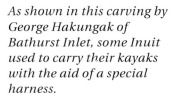

As shown in this carving by George Hakungak of Bathurst Inlet, some Inuit used to carry their kayaks with the aid of a special harness.

extremely strong and molds itself to skin and does not tear it. They worked and talked and laughed, drank gallons of very strong sweet tea, and at the end of the day the kayak was finished: long and elegant, sleek and buoyant, the most perfect hunting craft ever designed by man.

Captain George Best of Martin Frobisher's 1578 expedition to Meta Incognita, the unknown bourne — as Queen Elizabeth I had referred to Baffin Island — watched the Inuit's kayaks with a seaman's appreciation: "They haue boates made of leather, and couered cleane ouer, sauing one place in the middle to fit in… and they use to row therin with one Ore more swiftly a great deale, than we in our boates can doe with twentie."

The kayak's range was immense: 7,000 miles (11 200 km), from East Greenland to the east coast of Siberia, and to the Aleutian Islands (where the kayak was called *baidarka*). Although there were dozens of regional designs, the basic concept was the same throughout this entire range: a frame built of driftwood, bone, and ivory, covered with sealskins or, in a few inland cases, with caribou skins. Driftwood was common in Alaska but rare and precious in most other parts of the Arctic. Short pieces were skillfully scarfed and tenoned with treenails of wood or bone, and these joints were further strengthened with sealskin lashing.

Ekalun of Bathurst Inlet was about ten years old when he was "discovered" by European explorers. He was married before he had a gun (until then he hunted with bow and arrow). One autumn, he and I walked far inland, searching for caribou. At a river where caribou crossed during migration, we found old caches, tent rings, and the remains of a kayak. Seeing the ancient craft, its wood bleached but the lines still smooth and graceful, put the old hunter into a reminiscent mood. "We hid beneath the bank there," he said. "And when the caribou were in the river we rushed out with our kayaks and killed them with spears." His eyes gleamed with the relived excitement of long-ago hunts. The spears had been tipped with stone-hammered pieces of native copper. To build a kayak then, with stone tools, said Ekalun, took more than a month.

These women are sewing a sealskin cover for the kayak skeleton in the foreground of the photograph.

Ululik Duneq caches a narwhal tail and slabs of meat, skin, and fat to age and ferment for about a year.

Masautsiaq Eipe uses a spear-thrower, one of mankind's most ancient inventions, to harpoon a seal.

These inland craft used by the Umingmaktormiut, the Bathurst Inlet people, were light (less than 30 pounds [13.5 kg]), round-bottomed, and extremely cranky.

Qaivigarssuaq of the Polar Inuit vividly remembered these tippy kayaks. As a member of Knud Rasmussen's Fifth Thule Expedition (1921–24) he had made the greatest of all Arctic trips — three years and 30,000 miles (48 000 km) by dog team from Greenland to Alaska, with a side-trip to Siberia. At Bathurst Inlet, Qaivigarssuaq, then young and an expert kayaker, had stepped confidently into the light local craft and, to the joy of all, promptly overturned it. He smiled as he reminisced at Inerssussat. Now seventy-one years old, he was still one of the best, most active hunters in the Thule district. "There were many different types of kayaks with the people we visited," he recalled. "And now, I hear, all of them use other boats." I asked him about his epic three-year dog-team journey along the top of the world. "It was a fine trip," he said in typical Polar Inuit understatement.

Early in this century, visitors to settlements along Hudson Strait still spoke of "flotillas of kayaks." But first the whalers' sturdy whale boats and then the ubiquitous canoe imported from the south displaced the kayak. When the Canadian ethnologist Milton Freeman visited the Belcher Islands in Hudson Bay in 1961, all hunters, except two, used kayaks. When I lived on the Belcher Islands in 1968, only three kayaks were left. They were the last three kayaks used by hunters in the Canadian Arctic. These superb craft are still used in Greenland, but they have died out as hunting boats in Canada and Alaska.

ARCTIC MEAT

When I first went to stay with Inuit, for weeks and often for months, I had misgivings about living on meat alone. It was not what my culture considered a "balanced diet." Yet common sense told me that since the Inuit were healthy I, too, would be healthy if I ate the meat in their fashion, some cooked, some raw. This turned out to be true, and hunger quickly took care of my ingrained cultural aversion to eating raw meat.

Explorers died in droves of scurvy in regions where Inuit had prospered for thousands of years. The reason was diet: the Europeans lived on salt beef, and its lack of vitamins eventually killed them. The Inuit thrived on fresh meat. Many of their favorite animal parts are rich in vitamins: liver contains high amounts of vitamins A and D (polar-bear liver is so rich in vitamin A it is poisonous; if one eats it, one can die of hypervitaminosis); muktuk, the skin of whales, is very rich in vitamin C, richer per unit of weight than oranges.

But meat, raw or boiled, is bland. The Inuit found salt disgusting; their words for *salt* and *bitter sea water* are synonymous. So, to add zip to their diet, they fermented meat, a habit that horrified

Children await their father's return from the hunt.

southerners, who reported with disgust that Inuit ate "rotten" meat. Actually the relationship between rotten meat and fermented meat is roughly that between spoiled milk and cheese. And properly ripened meat tastes very much like cheese. A favorite after-dinner delicacy of the Bathurst Inlet people with whom I lived was *ingaluawinik*, caribou mesentery fat, pressed into a pouch and fermented for months until it tasted like Danish blue cheese — only more so.

The Inuit of Little Diomede Island in Bering Strait keep most of their food in meat holes — spacious, stone-lined caverns, some of great age, dug deep into the frozen mountainside. Their diet when I first lived with them in 1975 was still largely traditional, and the people were healthy. The main food was boiled seal or walrus meat. Blubber, aged until it was saffron-yellow and then marinated in seal oil, was eaten as a zesty condiment with the bland meat, or with *kauk*, boiled walrus skin, which is best after it has aged in a meat hole for about a year.

The real masters in the art of fermenting meat are the Polar Inuit. They use ancient stone caches in which the meat slowly ripens, and they are as finicky and concerned about these caches as the people of Roquefort are about the drafts and temperature in the ancient limestone caves in which their famous cheeses mature.

The result of this process is such delicacies as *iterssoraq*, year-old narwhal tail, slowly fermented in a blubber-lined rock cache, the skin bright green, the blubber olive green, the meat black and greenishly marbled, with the taste of the different parts ranging roughly from Brie to Roquefort to old Stilton; and, best loved by all, *kiviaq*, unplucked dovekies placed into blubber-lined sealskin bags and aged under rocks, untouched by direct sunlight, for about a year, until they have the pungent smell and flavor of old Gorgonzola.

In fall, I moved from Inerssussat up Inglefield Bay to the ancient narwhal hunting camp at Kangerdluqssuaq to live with a famous hunter, Ululik Duneq, and his family. As a gift, I took along from Qaanaaq a big chunk of very potent cheese. "Ah!" exclaimed Ululik as he tasted the cheese, "just like kiviaq!"

LABRADOR: WILD AND TRAGIC SHORES

A Labrador hunter harpoons a seal.

IN 1968, I CIRCUMNAVIGATED LABRADOR. IT WOULD HAVE BEEN easier if I had had a boat. Since I didn't have one, I made it in slow stages, from town to town, village to village, camp to camp, by whatever conveyance was available: coastal boats, cutters, fishing boats, Inuit canoes — much of it by Inuit canoes. I left Montreal at the end of winter and traveled east along the north shore of the Gulf of St. Lawrence, up the Labrador coast to its northernmost point, Killiniq Island with its now abandoned village of Port Burwell, then west along the coasts of Ungava Bay and Hudson Strait; finally, just ahead of winter, I headed south along the east coast of Hudson Bay and James Bay to Moosonee, where I had started my northern travels in the early 1950s, and from there, after six months and 5,000 miles (8000 km), by train back to Montreal. It was, a Polar Inuk would have said, "a fine trip."

In some ways it was also a sad trip, because the history of Labrador is haunted by tragedy. "This is the land God gave to Cain," wrote Jacques Cartier upon discovering the north shore of the Gulf of St. Lawrence in 1534. "It is composed of stones and horrible rugged rock… there is nothing but moss and short, stunted shrubs." The North Shore does have a distinctly east-of-Eden feeling, but it also has a marvelously wild grandeur and, at the time of Cartier, it was the home of Inuit who hunted, on the latitude of London, England, the then immensely numerous seals and whales. These southernmost of all Inuit then ranged as far south and west as the present North Shore town of Havre-Saint-Pierre, which, until 1925, was called Pointe-aux-Esquimaux.

The "conquest" of the Arctic, unlike most other conquests, was generally a peaceful one: the explorers explored, the traders traded, the whalers whaled. But none planned to settle in the cold and barren North and, since economic interests did not collide, fights with Inuit were rare. Addressing his land, a Greenland Inuk said in 1756: "How well it is that, if in your rocks there are gold and silver, for which the Christians are so greedy, it is covered with so much snow that they cannot get at it! Your unfruitfulness makes us happy and saves us from molestation!"

When interests did collide, the Natives suffered. Siberia's

promyshlenniki, the fur hunters, responded instantly in 1742 to reports of sea-otter wealth on the just-discovered Aleutian Islands. They were a breed of northern conquistador — greedy, rowdy, brave, brutal. They robbed and enslaved the Aleuts and sent cargo after cargo of sea-otter pelts back to Siberia. Imperial ukases from faraway St. Petersburg thundered in vain against "such barbarities, plunder, and ravaging of women." In a few decades, the once-proud Aleuts had been reduced from an estimated 16,000 to a broken, subservient remnant of barely 2,000.

In newly discovered Canada, cod was king. The seas bordering Labrador were then stupendously rich in fish. John Cabot reported in 1497 that cod swam in layers so thick no nets were needed to catch them. They could be scooped up with weighted wicker baskets. The St. Lawrence, wrote Cartier, "is the richest [river] in every kind of fish that anyone remembers ever having seen or heard of."

On these coasts, the Inuit were in the way. They were feared and hated by the fishermen, and usually shot on sight. The prevailing feeling of European fishermen was summed up by Samuel de Champlain, founder of New France, when he wrote about the Inuit in 1632: "For the most part they are small men… wicked and treacherous in the highest degree. They clothe themselves in the skins of seals… their boats are of leather. In them they go prowling about and making war. The origin of this war was the killing — accidentally or otherwise — of a wife of a chief of this nation by one of the St. Malo sailors."

The odds were against the Inuit. By 1766, 1,500 European vessels with 15,000 men caught fish off the south Labrador coast. At that time, the total Inuit population of Labrador was estimated at 3,000. The Inuit were exterminated on the Gulf of St. Lawrence coast and pushed farther and farther north.

In 1766, to end this warfare and protect the remaining Inuit, Admiral Sir Hugh Palliser, governor of Newfoundland, accepted the offer of German missionaries, the Moravian Brethren (already established among the Inuit of Greenland), to found missions along the Labrador coast. The Moravians demanded, and after some hedging got, 100,000 acres (40 000 ha) to go with each mission established, a sort of *cordon sanitaire* to keep the European fishermen away from their flock, and gave their missions German or Old Testament names: Hoffenthal (now Hopedale), Zoar, Nain, Ramah, Hebron.

Most of the missionaries were smiths, carpenters, farmers, coopers, or bookkeepers. They were pious but practical, immensely industrious, and totally devoted to "their" people and their work. Most came as young men and women and left after twenty, thirty, even forty years of service (at £15 to £25 per annum, from which they had to supply their own clothing, breakfast, and "incidentals"). They built big European-style houses on the rugged, rocky coast of Labrador and heated them with large cast-iron stoves, but the cold was so intense and the buildings so poorly insulated that "the walls are all winter covered with ice, and the bed clothes freeze to the wall." For more than 150 years, the Moravians kept detailed diaries at all mission stations, a fascinating record of life on the Labrador coast a long time ago.

I lived for a while at the mission in Hopedale and read there the diaries, the older ones great vellum-bound volumes, kept in meticulous Gothic script. They spoke of hope and hunger, of hardship and happiness, of Inuit collecting eider eggs in early summer (as many as 2,500 eggs per day), of the salads of summer grown in lovingly prepared beds, of Inuit seal hunts at the *sinna*, the floe edge, of rendering seal oil for sale to Europe, and of waiting with intense longing for the brief annual visit of the mission ship, their only contact with "home."

The anthropologist E.W. Hawkes, who visited Labrador in 1914, concluded that the Inuit "are not immoral or moral, they are simply natural." They were often a good deal too "natural" for the somewhat straitlaced missionaries. One man who had many wives refused to give them up, explaining "he needed them to row his boat," for the large open *umiak* was traditionally rowed by women and was known in the eastern Arctic as the "women's boat."

Sarah Millie bakes bread in a stove made from a cut-down drum. She uses driftwood for fuel.

The diaries dwelt often, sadly, and at length, on moral lapses. In Hopedale, one man, accused of having "sinned," cheerfully confessed and submitted a long list of women with whom he had sinned. The women excused their behavior by saying they did it only to revenge themselves on their gallivanting husbands, some of them church elders. At the end of this three-page entry, the diarist seemed to sigh: "The weather has been unfavorable for drying fish lately."

Each ship that touched these isolated people could bring illnesses to which they had little or no immunity. Like a somber leitmotiv, tales of disease and death run through the diaries:

> Okak 1850. Fifty Inuit die in an epidemic.
>
> Hebron 1863. Fifty people die in six months.
>
> Nain 1864. Thirteen births; 31 deaths.
>
> Nain 1894. Close to 100 people die out of a population of 250.
>
> Nain 1902. At the death of a child: "We were sorry to hear of his loss, as this is the last of 13 children his wife had borne."
>
> Hopedale 1907. "There is no doubt of the sad fact that the Eskimo race is dying out in Labrador."
>
> Okak 1917. Measles kill 44. "Tuberculosis, too, is making rapid progress among our people."

And finally, the dreadful coda: the 1918 Spanish flu epidemic. A sick sailor aboard the mission supply ship *Harmony* carried the disease from one Labrador settlement to the next. In Hebron, "in the course of nine days two-thirds of the population were corpses." At Okak, 215 died out of a population of 263. Not a single adult male survived. Within three months, more than a third of all Labrador Inuit were dead.

On Sundays, I would go to church in Nain. The German Brethren have long ago left the Labrador coast; most ministers now are from England. But echoes of the 200-year Inuit-German association persist: traits, words, names. There was, especially among the older men, a German *Tüchtigkeit*, a Teutonic love for precision, order, and time, tempered by the Inuit's traditional dislike and disregard for such things.

Until the Germans came, the Inuit of Labrador (and most other Inuit) would count only to five or six. Anything beyond that was simply "many"; exactitude was not important to them. Now they count in precise German: "*eins, zwei, drei...*" Their year was traditionally divided into seasons, the seasons into approximate months: February was *Koblut*, ground-cracked-by-frost month; June was *Munilut*, egg month; July *Kitujialut*, mosquito month; and September *Qononilut*, the fading month, when fall colors died

At his fishing camp on an island off Hopedale, Labrador, Joe Millik makes a new net.

A father and his daughter in the Moravian church in Nain, Labrador.

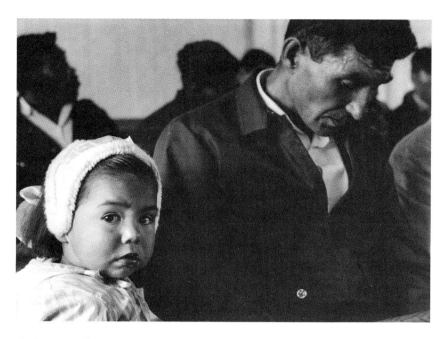

and winter began. But their month had no weeks, and days had no names, so on the coast of Labrador, Inuit use German-derived names for weekdays: *Sontageme, Montageme, Denestageme, Mitwokeme, Donestageme, Fraitageme, Sonabendeme.* And many adopted missionary names: one Inuk I met was Johannes Kohlmeister, another Nikodemus Mentzel.

The Inuit also inherited the German missionaries' love for music. They made an early (about 1800) and apparently effortless transition from their own music with its simple pentatonic scale to the complex harmonies of Bach. As the presiding church elder, Martin Martin, dressed in white shirt, blue suit, and sealskin boots, came to the end of the service, the antiphonal chant of the congregation soared "*heilig, heilig, heilig* (holy, holy, holy)," and they sang in Inuktitut, with deep love, feeling, and perfect harmony, the grand chorales of Bach.

From Nain I traveled on in the *Killinek*, the boat that took supplies to the fishing camps in the far-northern fiords. The captain was Joshua Obed, a small wiry man with few teeth and a crinkly, friendly smile. He was all efficiency and drive: we stopped briefly at each camp; unloaded bags of salt, letters, and other supplies; loaded barrels of salted char; gave a long blast with the hand-held foghorn; and were off to the next camp. There were no stops for tea and tales, and I was usually not allowed ashore because he assumed, correctly, that photographers have a tendency to stray and are hard to round up again.

But Joshua was very kind and a wonderful teacher. He deeply loved this wild and lonely land and knew every bay and bight, run and rattle, turn and tickle of the complex coast, which was as well, for he never used maps, and both his compass and his radio were broken.

Jefta Jararuse, a Labrador hunter and fisherman.

Nowhere, not in southern Chile or northern Norway, have I ever seen such a magnificent coast: deep fiords, soaring mountains, a majestic loneliness and wildness, an empty land. After the devastation of disease and the lack of mission funds, all villages north of Nain were abandoned. Only stones and rubble, overgrown with moss and grass, remain of Ramah (named after the town in Judah where the prophet Samuel was born). This was once the Inuit's Olympus, home of their god Torngarsoak, after whom the Torngat Mountains are named.

At night, we anchored off Okak. Joshua rowed me ashore and returned at once to the ship. To the Inuit it is a haunted place, a place of death and fear and ghosts, and there was an oppressive feeling of sadness as I walked among the ruins of the long-abandoned village in the soft gray light of the northern night. When the disease struck, Joshua told me, people fled the cursed village to remote wilderness camps. But they took the disease with them and died in lonely agony, and the unfed sled dogs ate the corpses. At one camp, only a five-year-old girl survived. The ravenous dogs tried to kill her, but one husky defended her. For three weeks the faithful animal protected the little girl, fighting off all the other dogs. When rescuers finally came, the husky was weak and exhausted, but it would let no one near the girl, and finally the faithful dog had to be shot.

At another camp, a cabin on the coast, all died except, again, one young girl. She did not dare to leave the cabin and lived mainly on water and raw flour. When rescuers finally arrived, they saw the

A member of Nain's brass band practices. Labrador Inuit inherited their love of music from German missionaries.

girl's white, flour-smeared face at the window and fled in terror. "There is only a ghost in that camp," they told the missionaries, who immediately rushed north to the camp. The girl, after more than a month alone in that dreadful cabin with the decaying bodies of her family, was alive, and now, forty years later, still lived on the Labrador coast.

At Hebron, we stopped to take on water. We were ahead of Joshua's demanding schedule, and here he came ashore with me. We filled our 5-gallon (18-l) plastic jugs with water from a bright, rushing brook, flanked by dense willow and alder. Poor Joshua! This had once been his home. "No people now," he said sadly. "This was a good place. Lots of seals. Lots of fish. Lots of caribou!" He stopped at a small mound, intensely green; voles scurried through the dense grass. Long ago, his house had stood here.

Other buildings still survived: the great church, prefabricated in Germany and erected here in 1832, the entire building raised several feet above the ground on four gigantic oak pillars — perhaps the earliest architectural attempt to cope with the problems of permafrost; the long-shuttered mission, with its broad central corridor, once the playground of towheaded German children, constructed with 44,900 bricks shipped from Europe; barns; greenhouses; a dark, soot-stained building still permeated with the sickly-sweet smell of rancid blubber, where "train oil" was once rendered from seal and whale carcasses.

Around the long-abandoned buildings a profusion of bright poppies, red, yellow, orange, and white, nodded in the chill Labrador breeze. They had been brought from Europe more than a century ago, and lovingly planted and nurtured by homesick missionaries. As we walked through the empty village, two rough-legged hawks rose from their nearby nest and circled above us with wild and mournful cries.

We went far inland on the great Saglek Fiord. Sheer cliffs, stratified in red and brown and black, in cream and sienna and madder, soared 2,000 feet (600 m) and more from the blue-black water of the fiord. Snowfields sparkled in the sun; lacy waterfalls cascaded down the cliffs. Several Inuit families were camped at the head of the fiord, living in the large, strong, white canvas tents that are now the summer homes of so many Inuit families from Alaska to East Greenland when they return for weeks and often for months "to live again on the land," as they say.

"Can I stay with you?" I asked Tom Okuatsiak.

"Sure," he said.

Then he had a worrying thought. "Do you eat fish?" he asked, and, when I said yes, he looked relieved and said, "Stay as long as you like." Our food for the next weeks was mainly fish and bannock, the unleavened bread made in a pan, introduced long ago by Scots traders and now part of the Inuit language and staple Inuit

A rainbow arcs over Saglek Fiord, Labrador, as Tom Okuatsiak cleans char.

fare. Occasionally we had seal and bannock, and once, when someone shot a black bear, bear and bannock.

Our camp was comfortable. The tent was large, we slept on cots, and on rainy days the camp stove, a cut-down 45-gallon (170-l) drum, glowed. Tom was a tall, powerful man, with close-cropped hair and a dark, rather stern face, but soft-spoken and gentle. Martha, his wife, was warm and motherly; she loved to feed us. "Eat more!" she urged at every meal, and stuffed more fish into Maggy, the fat baby she had recently adopted from a neighbor whose husband had drowned in a storm. The two boys, Tom and Amadeus, played endlessly, and teenager Mary, disturbingly beautiful in T-shirt and stretch pants, helped her mother, played with the baby, or listened to badly scratched records on the old hand-cranked phonograph.

It was a pleasant, timeless life. Tom rose early, rowed to his nets, took out all the char, and then joined us for a breakfast of fish and bannock. It often rained. Tom, undisturbed, would cut up, clean, and wash the fish before salting them away in barrels. Between storms and wild black clouds, brilliant rainbows arched across the fiord.

At night, Tom reminisced. He had grown up on the Ungava coast in a region without stores, and young men had walked across the mountains with sacks of fur to exchange at the store in Hebron for flour, sugar, tea, tobacco, traps, and ammunition. They had then returned through the mountain wilderness, each man carrying a load of from 100 to 150 pounds (45 to 67.5 kg), a round trip of more than a month. He spoke of *sapotit* (stone fishing weirs), of spearing char with leisters, of intricate traps and snares used long ago, of heating winter homes with *kudlit* (seal-oil lamps) — and Mary, who had grown up in Nain and had gone to school in Newfoundland, listened in wonder, for this was to her an unknown world.

One dark night in early August a cry went up: "A ship! A ship!" We dashed out of the tent, and a gigantic apparition from another world, lights twinkling in the night, slid cautiously into our fiord and the anchor rattled down. We rowed over. It was a Canadian Coast Guard ship. The crew were unmistakably Quebeckers and I called to them in French. "*Dis-donc!*" said a surprised voice in the darkness. "*Les Esquimaux ici parlent français!*" They had come to buy fresh fish from the Natives, were fascinated that I should live with them, and asked politely but very curiously all the standard questions: Did Tom share his wife with me? Did they eat only blubber? and when I told them how we lived, they lost all interest. Old tales and preconceived ideas are sacred and have a life of their own.

When we ran out of tobacco some weeks later, the whole family went by fishing boat to the DEW Line station 50 miles (80 km)

Sporting dramatic homemade goggles, Sarah Millik eats lunch during a 1968 trip to a fishing camp on the Labrador coast.

away, where a white radar dome perched like a giant's golf ball atop 2,000-foot (610-m)-high Cape Uivik at the entrance to Saglek Fiord. We remained to see a film, a fairly silly science-fiction story of a California family that buys a dream house in the suburbs. At first all is wonderful, but the house is haunted: a poltergeist slams doors and knocks things off tables, and then evil spirits take over and the real terror begins.

Our flat-bottomed, diesel-powered boat tuck-tuck-tuckered through the night, Tom at the tiller, the family sleeping peacefully, huddled together in the bottom of the open boat. Tom was pensive. Something worried him, and after a while he asked. Tom understood, of course, that the film had been part fact, part supernatural. His problem was that he did not know where fact ended and fiction began. For Tom, who had never been away from the Labrador coast, all California seemed like science fiction.

The soft glow of morning spread over the sky and mirrored the mountains in a shining sea. In the distance, a few white specks beneath the soaring cliffs, were the tents of our camp. The kids stretched and yawned; Maggy, hungry, began to cry. Tom went to check his nets. Martha lit the stove and made breakfast. Mary shushed and fed the baby. The sun rose above the mountains and flooded our valley with golden light, and camp life resumed its ancient rhythm.

FISHING, CLAMMING, CRABBING

It is almost as though the Inuit in former days were following God's injunction to Noah that "every moving thing that liveth shall be meat for you," and caught, killed, and ate anything, from 2-ounce (56-g) lemmings to 60-ton (54-tonne) bowhead whales.

By far the most important animals to them, however, were seals and caribou, the *sine qua non* of their life in the Arctic. Had God created the world with only these two animals, the Inuit would have been content, for seals and caribou supplied them with most of their food and clothing.

Some groups specialized: the people of Little Diomede Island in Bering Strait are primarily walrus hunters. The Inuit of the Mackenzie Delta region hunted white whales, and still do. The inland Inuit had no seals; they lived mainly on caribou and fish, and obtained durable sealskins (for boot soles) and seal oil (for their stone lamps) in trade from coastal people.

There were no caribou in a few Arctic regions. They died out on

A fisherman of Little Diomede Island hauls up crabs from the icy water of Bering Strait.

Early morning at the char fishing camp at the head of Saglek Fiord.

the Belcher Islands in Hudson Bay in the 1880s when an abnormal winter rain was followed by heavy frost and the islands were covered with a hard, glittering carapace of ice. The caribou could not dig through it for food, and all starved to death. Deprived of caribou pelts for winter clothing, the ingenious Inuit made them from eider-duck skins. A *mitvin*, an eider-duck parka, was as warm as a caribou parka, but not as lasting.

In addition to vital seal and caribou, nearly all Inuit caught fish, from small, bony sculpins to huge Greenland sharks, whose toxic meat could be eaten only by people who knew how to prepare it. The Inuit had nets: in the Bering Sea region they used large nets of seal or walrus thong to capture seals, and even whales. In Greenland, the English explorer John Davis saw in 1586 nets made of baleen: "They [the Inuit] make nets to take their fish of the finne of the whale." (Siberia's Chukchi, close neighbors of the Inuit, wove their nets of nettle fibers.) The most common way, though, to capture fish was with hook and line, or with leisters.

The most important, most delicious fish was char, once infinitely numerous in lakes and rivers and the sea. Unlike its close cousin, the salmon, the char does not jump. Taking advantage of this, Inuit built sapotit across rivers, often in rocky rapids, with an entrance sluice leading to a central, rock-surrounded basin. Once the basin was swarming with ascending fish, the Inuit closed the low stone weir, jumped into the icy water, and speared the char with three-pronged leisters. It was numbingly cold, but wildly exciting: the women screaming on shore, the children jumping on the rocks, and then great feasts of fish, and rocks covered with blood-red split char, drying for the coming winter.

Octave Sivanertok of Repulse Bay, on the northwest coast of Hudson Bay, took me along in spring to fish for char and lake trout. He drove his powerful snowmobile with speed and consummate skill. The long sled, pulled by ropes, rattled and hammered over rock-hard snow and ice ridges, and often slewed wildly. I got a merciless pounding and had to hang on like a limpet to avoid being tossed off when the sled caromed off ice blocks. With the snowmobile, Arctic travel gained in speed but lost most of its romance and comfort. Traveling by dog team, leisurely and silent, was usually a pleasure. One was aware of land and frozen sea, and felt as one with it. But it was slow. Octave covered in hours what would have taken days with a dog team.

We stopped for the night near a frozen lake. Octave built an igloo, wind-proof and much warmer than a tent. He chiseled a hole through the 6-foot (2-m)-thick ice of the lake, built a windbreak of snow blocks, and jigged for lake trout. I went for a long walk to relax my battered bottom. When I returned, the last rays of the setting sun slanted across land and lake and flecked the snow with nacre and gold. Octave, endlessly patient, still jigged for trout. A row of speckled, bronze-glistening fish lay near him.

Next day we crossed Tesserssuaq, the big lake, and finally came to Sapotit Lake, really a series of lakes connected by shallow, fast-flowing rivers. Dark water welled up and poured in milky-turquoise streamers across the ice. Here, in summers long ago, men caught char at sapotit. Many of the ancient stone weirs still existed, but were breached to let the migrating fish pass. Now many Inuit had come, like us, from Repulse Bay to spear fish with leisters. They kneeled at the edge of the ice, jigged metal lures with metronome regularity (in former days the lures were of carved ivory or polished bone), held leisters poised, and peered intently into the crystal-clear water for the golden flash of trout or the silver and rose of char. A lightning thrust, and the fish, held firmly by the leister prongs, was pulled onto the ice. Some leisters were still made of musk-ox horn, the best traditional material, strong and flexible. New leister tines were carved from the strong, thick plastic used for the counters of butcher shops. Sapotit and leisters are among mankind's oldest inventions. Magdalenian hunters used them 30,000 years ago during the final Paleolithic culture in western Europe.

Clams, where available, are a favorite food for Inuit. Some come already collected and even a bit predigested. At Little Diomede Island in Bering Strait, walrus hunters took 50 pounds (22.5 kg) and more of recently shucked clams from the stomach of each walrus they killed. Masses of these clams were eaten fresh, raw or cooked, and more were slipped onto strings and air-dried for future use. In 1975, when I first lived on Little Diomede, I tried to improve on this by making clam chowder and invited Inuit friends to my shack for supper. But the clams, soaked in walrus gastric

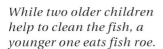

While two older children help to clean the fish, a younger one eats fish roe.

With his three-pronged leister at hand, Octave Sivanertok jigs for fish with an ivory lure in the spring of 1974.

Masautsiaq and Sofie Eipe and their grandson gaff Greenland halibut from a lead in the spring of 1971.

juices, curdled the milk, and the chowder, like nearly all my cooking, was a disaster. When I returned fifteen years later to live again on Little Diomede, it was still remembered. "Have you come back to make more chowder?" someone asked.

At Aberdeen Bay on the north shore of Hudson Strait, which the Inuit call Taksertoot, the place of fogs, we had to dig our own clams. Inuit from the settlements of Lake Harbour and Cape Dorset also gather at this remote bay to quarry with pickaxes, chisels, sledgehammers, and crowbars the distinctive jade-green soapstone for which their superb carvings are famous.

Hunting in Inuit society is man's work. Both men and women fish. But clam digging, berry picking, and egg collecting are usually family affairs, and Inuit often make it into a joyous outing.

At Bathurst Inlet, racks of char dry in the sun, food for the coming winter.

Tents glow at night at Aberdeen Bay, Hudson Strait, where Inuit fish and clam, as well as mine the famous jade-green soapstone they use for their sculptures.

Matthew Kellypallik of Cape Dorset saw me on the beach and called: "You want to come along?" (I had dropped broad hints in camp that I wanted to go on a clamming trip), and we were off, a large canoe full of happy people, two pet dogs, and lots of zinc and plastic pails. We drove to a far bay and, as the tide (here more than 30 feet [9 m] high) receded, walked out onto the great mud flats and dug for clams with spoons, forks, knives, or sticks, most soon bent or broken. Some clams were huge — hand-long and perhaps forty or fifty years old. There are few walruses on this coast, and humans rarely visit; most clams can grow and age in peace. An

CHAPTER FOUR

JOURNEY TO THE SAVAGE ISLANDS

CHANGE CAME SLOWLY TO THE ARCTIC. LIFE FLOWED SEAMLESSLY from generation to generation: traditions were treasured and passed on; legends memorized and told and retold by the soft yellow light of seal-oil lamps during long winter evenings; sons learned hunting skills and the lore of the land by hunting with their fathers; girls learned early from their mothers how to sew the vital Arctic clothing and played endlessly with the children of the camp.

The archaeologist Moreau S. Maxwell of Michigan State University worked near Lake Harbour on southern Baffin Island and he invited me to the site where he and his assistants were removing, with trowels, brushes, and infinite patience, layer after layer of earth and bones, century after century of human habitation. At one ancient house site, they had reached a level dating 1,000 years ago. Maxwell drew a ground plan and I recognized it instantly. It was quite similar to the living patterns used in Inuit homes until recently. Where the lady of the house had sat and tended her oil lamp a thousand years ago, the earth was oily black and smelled of ancient seal oil.

This site, Maxwell explained, had been continuously occupied for at least 4,000 years. Pre-Dorset people hunted here when Babylon was built. About 100 to 150 people lived then in eight to ten camps along this coast of Baffin Island. For nearly 2,000 years the same sites were occupied by Dorset-culture people, the giant Tunit of Inuit legends and tales. And after them this coast was home to about 250 Thule-culture Inuit in ten or twelve camps.

They lived in sealskin tents in summer and in winter in igloos or in *qarmait*, houses built with whalebone or driftwood rafters, covered with animal skins, and well insulated with dried heather and ample layers of snow. The anthropologist Franz Boas lived with the Baffin Island Inuit in 1883 and 1884 and found "this kind of hut… very warm, light and comfortable." The population, in balance with the resources of land and sea, varied little during four millennia. It was about 250 in 1957.

In 1957, the Inuit of the Lake Harbour region lived in eleven camps at ancient, traditional sites along more than 300 miles (480 km) of coastline. They used canvas tents in summer, and igloos or qarmait in winter. They dressed in caribou-skin clothing and traveled by dog team, and nearly all their food came from sea and land. Two or three times a year they went to Lake Harbour to trade

A young mother collects berries in the fall.

furs for guns, ammunition, traps, sugar, tea, and tobacco at the Hudson's Bay Company post (established in 1911) and visited the Anglican mission (established in 1909). A ship with supplies came once a year, and the RCMP made patrols by dog team and visited all the camps. Contact with the outside world was minimal.

But suddenly change did come to this ancient world, total change, and it came with dizzying speed and abruptness. The Canadian government built a school in Lake Harbour, and houses for teachers and administrators. Houses were also built for the Inuit, and they were urged to move to town, where their children now went to school. By 1968, ten of the eleven camps had vanished; the people had left the land.

One man refused to budge. Ooloopie Killiktee remained at Kiijuak, the camp close to Hudson Strait where he grew up, and some members of his clan remained with him on the land.

In Lake Harbour I lived with Bee Lyta, a mild-mannered bachelor with a house and space to spare. Lake Harbour was pleasant and peaceful and appeared prosperous. Most men and many women were good carvers. Their work and income gave them pride and independence, and Lake Harbour was not haunted by the devastating uselessness and boredom of near-total unemployment among the young that is the curse of many Arctic communities. A few Inuit were famous carvers whose works were eagerly bought, at top prices, by galleries, collectors, and museums. They made a lot of money and spent it easily. The year before I was in Lake Harbour one man flew quietly to Montreal, bought beautiful furniture, and glowed in the general envy and the ohs and ahs when the supply ship arrived with it in Lake Harbour in fall. A piqued neighbor promptly flew to Montreal, bought furniture that was dramatically ostentatious, and had it airlifted, at fabulous cost, to Lake Harbour.

I sent a radio message to Killiktee and asked whether I could live at his camp. The reply was a cautious *imaha*, maybe, and a few days later his son-in-law, Josephee Padluq, came to town to look me over

A large herd of caribou migrates north across the tundra.

and to ascertain just how much of a problem I was likely to be. To ask direct questions is impolite in Inuit society. Josephee, however, was used to whites and was quite blunt: Would I pay for staying at camp? Did I have suitable clothing? And, most important: Did I eat Inuit food? He knew of me. "You're the man that lives with Inuit," he said. We drank more tea and then he left.

A few days later, while we were eating supper and talking of this and that, Bee Lyta suddenly said, "Tomorrow I take you to camp." It was a total surprise; such decisions always were. There had been talk, there had been radio messages, but no one spoke to me and when I asked they shrugged and said, "*Achoo* (I do not know.)"

It was only 30 miles (48 km) to Killiktee's camp, a quick ride by snowmobile and sled on early summer ice. According to government records, Killiktee was seventy-one years old. His children thought he was "about sixty years old." When I asked Killiktee, he shrugged and smiled. "*Nauna* (I do not know)," he said. And he did not care. "We did not count years when I was young," he explained.

Dressed in a double-layered caribou-skin suit, an Inuk hunter can be comfortably warm at -58º F (-50º C).

With his weather-darkened, strong-boned face and thick thatch of jet-black hair, Killiktee looked stern and aloof, like a haughty Inca noble. But he was really a kindly man who liked to joke and laugh, a gentle patriarch — for all in camp were members of his family: daughters, a son, a son-in-law, an adopted son, and a horde of happy grandchildren.

Until 1977, they spent winters in the ancient qarmait. That year the government had given to this "outpost camp" four one-room, double-walled plywood houses, known as "matchbox houses" in the North. Three were satisfactory. The fourth house, unfortunately, was haunted, Joe Ahme told me. He was Killiktee's nephew and was spending some weeks on the land before joining the Canadian army. "There was a ghost in the house," he said. "It laugh like crazy all the time." They poured gasoline on the floor, threw in a match, and burned both house and ghost.

Camp life seems chaotic; at first it always bothers me. I'm an orderly person, meticulous and methodical (infuriatingly so, says my wife). I have a linear mind that, in due time, progresses from A to B to C, and abrupt zigs and zags from established routine fill me with angst. I make lists of "what to do today" and fret if things do not get done. I'm ten minutes early for all appointments, and despite a lifetime of travel, I'm at the airport at least two hours before plane departure.

Camp life is not at all like that. There is no fixed time for anything, no routine, no apparent order. All seem to do as they please, when it pleases them. The men may hunt, or carve, or sleep, or talk. The children sleep half the day, then play far into the night. The women sew, bake bannock, drink tea and talk, or fuss over babies — their own or anyone else's, for children are deeply loved.

But there is a certain ancient rhythm to camp life, a rhythm that goes back to the beginnings of human existence, long before agriculture, animal husbandry, and eventually town life, with their demands for ordered time, fettered the once-free hunter. Mood, need, and weather regulated our lives. And moods were often contagious.

Shorty Killiktee, Killiktee's son, then already a well-known carver and now world-famous (several of his magnificent carvings were in the exhibition "Contemporary Inuit Masterworks," first at the United Nations in New York, and then at the "Earth Summit" during the summer of 1992 in Rio de Janeiro), took a big piece of soapstone, knelt in front of it, and looked carefully at it. He turned it, tapped it, studied it, looked pensive for a while, and suddenly the stone spoke to him and he saw in it the finished carving. He roughed out the carving with a hatchet, then chipped patiently at the rock with a welder's hammer and total assurance, following the dictates of his inner vision. The finished carving would be worth several thousand dollars.

Early morning fog at Ooloopie Killiktee's camp on Hudson Strait.

Josephee readied snowmobile and sled and drove to the floe edge to hunt seals. Killiktee followed, with a sled, me, and two grandsons in tow. An hour later, Shorty joined us at the floe edge. The men hunted for days; that was the mood of the camp. The magnificent sculpture stood half finished on the beach while Shorty shot seals whose pelts were worth about twenty dollars each. But hunting was life and passion, the very basis of their existence, their culture. Carving, generally, was work.

Killiktee was forever busy, hunting, carving, skinning seals, and repairing boats and hunting gear. His 22-foot (7-m) freighter canoe had been damaged the previous year. Now he began to repair it, with simple tools, great skill, and infinite patience and perseverance. Cracked strakes were strengthened with carefully planed and carved boards, salvaged from abandoned packing crates in Lake Harbour.

Intermittently, when they felt like it, two of his grandsons, Simeonie, six, and Eeshiak, thirteen, "helped" with the work. They sawed some boards, not very straight, hammered in nails but forgot to clinch them, and broke a drill. Killiktee never lost patience. He showed them again and again how to do it properly, rarely scolded them and often praised them, and, as the days passed, their skills improved noticeably.

We slept when we were tired, be it day or night; ate when we were hungry; and worked when we felt like working. We lived by mood and need, not measured time, and somehow things got done and we always had plenty to eat. Nearly every day, any time between four in the afternoon and four in the morning, most of the people in camp drifted toward Killiktee's house for a communal meal. His daughters, Simata and Akeego (his wife had died some

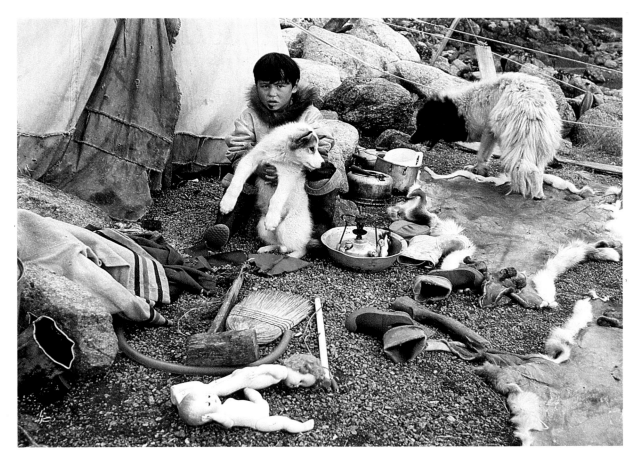

A boy plays with a husky pup at an Inuit hunting camp on Baffin Island in 1967.

Nooshoota sews a new tent for the trip to the Savage Islands. Her son, Pee, dresses the baby.

years before), boiled huge pots of seal meat, or ducks, or clams, or we simply lugged a seal inside and ate it raw together with boiled seaweed, a quick and healthy meal. We knelt around the seal, our hands and faces red with blood. Looking down upon this primeval scene were two huge wall posters: one of Elvis Presley in glittering finery, the other of a scantily clad girl riding upon a smiling tiger.

In May and early June, the men carved or hunted seals at the floe edge. In mid-June, the talk in camp turned to Pikyoolak, those faraway islands that are covered with eider-duck nests and that European explorers called the Savage Islands. This would be the great trip of our summer and the camp was alive with excitement and preparations. Nooshoota, Killiktee's daughter, sewed a large new canvas tent. Her husband, Josephee, traveled by snowmobile to Lake Harbour across early summer ice so water-carved and rotten, only saints, fools, or very experienced Inuit would dare to cross it. He returned with drums of gasoline, cases of motor oil, boxes of soft drinks, plenty of ammunition, two big bags of flour, and a carton of hardtack, which the Inuit of this coast call *seebaw*, a corruption of the German word *zwieback*, a term picked up from nineteenth-century whalers.

The Savage Islands now lie remote and forgotten off a rarely visited coast. But for nearly three centuries Inuit and Europeans held there, as Lieutenant Edward Chapell of the Royal Navy observed in 1814, "a sort of annual fair." The Inuit brought furs, oil, baleen, ivory carvings, and "unicorn's horn" (narwhal tusks); the Europeans arrived with metal objects, beads, cloth, and "European toys." Then, upon the ice near the islands, according to explorer G.F. Lyon in 1821, "a most noisy but merry barter instantly took place." When the trading was finished, the ship's fiddler went on the ice and "in a short time everyone on the floe, officers, men, and savages were dancing together."

The choice of the remote and bleak Savage Islands as the annual meeting place between Inuit and Europeans was determined by ice, currents, and prevailing winds. Noted Chapell: "Entering Hudson's Strait it is a necessary precaution to keep close in with the northern shore… since currents and ice in the south entrance are unfavorable and dangerous." Henry Hudson, his 55-ton (50-tonne) ship *Discovery* beset by wind and ice, sought shelter among the Savage Islands in 1610, but found them "a most barren place, having nothing on it but plashes of water and riven rock."

Five years later, William Baffin and Robert Bylot, again in the faithful *Discovery*, eased their way through pack ice along the north shore of Hudson Strait. On June 8, 1615, they reached a "company of islands… which after we called the Savage Isles." They landed upon one of the islands and saw there "tents and boats, with a number of dogs." But the people fled. Climbing a nearby hill,

A hunter scans the ice for game from atop a wave-sculptured iceberg.

Baffin spotted at sea "a great canoe [umiak] having about 14 persons in it…" Explorers and Natives waved to each other and made friendly signs, but the Inuit were "fearful of us, and we not willing to trust them," so they did not meet.

Near the Natives' sealskin tents, Baffin found a few "whale fins" (baleen) and a small bag containing "little images of men, and one the image of a woman with a child at her back, all of which I brought away," leaving knives, beads, and counters in exchange.

Thus barter began on the Savage Islands in 1615 and it soon became an annual event, keenly anticipated by Europeans and Inuit alike. From then on, as hundreds of ships passed into Hudson Bay, carrying traders, explorers, adventurers, missionaries, whalers, and naval personnel of several nations, most stopped at the Savage Islands. Nowhere else did Inuit and Europeans meet as regularly and over such a long period.

Among them was "Henry Ellis, Gent.," agent aboard the *Dobbs*, one of the many English ships searching for a short route to China and the wealth of the Orient, and stopping, first of all, at the Savage Islands. It was July 8, 1746, and as the ship anchored off the islands, three umiaks and twenty-six kayaks approached, full of Inuit "whose business was to trade." The Inuit brought baleen and sealskins and received hatchets, saws, and gimlets. "Their Stock was not great, but we made a considerable Profit from our Dealings with them," wrote Ellis. The Inuit, Ellis found, were "very cheerful and sprightly," but not overly impressed by Europeans. "They are extremely, I might say, obstinately attached to their own Customs and Manner of living…"

The ships stopped calling long ago, and the Inuit left the islands. But, once a year, when ice permitted, Killiktee and his clan visited the isolated islands to collect eider eggs, as Inuit from this coast had done for hundreds, perhaps thousands, of years. I knew the currents of our camp: soon we would leave. But when? I asked, infuriatingly often, no doubt, and was fed on "*Achoo.* (I do not know.)" and "*Imaha kaupat.* (Maybe tomorrow.)" And so it came that I was far from camp, watching a plover on its nest, when I heard Simata yell. She rushed up, wildly excited. "We go," she panted. "Hurry, hurry!"

Camp seemed utter chaos. The 30-foot (9-m)-high tide was in, the three big canoes were nearly level with the top of the ice foot, the broad belt of tide-formed ice that covers the coast. Women and children lugged belongings and provisions to the boats; the men stowed drums of gas. Pups got underfoot and yelped; kids found long-lost treasures; the baby had to be changed and fed; a pot of seal meat boiled on the beach; Eeshiak shot at herring gulls with his .22, and bullets zinged off the ice. But, in an hour, all was done. The boats were packed and we were off to the Savage Islands: nine adults; twelve children, including the baby; and pet dogs and pups.

We poled and pushed the boats through fields of broken ice. Once in the open water of Hudson Strait, the men started the outboard motors and we purred smoothly eastward along the rugged coast of Baffin Island. We traveled without halt all day, all night, and most of the following day. We cooked in the boats, ate in the boats, slept in the boats.

It was June 26, my fiftieth birthday. It was cold and clear. There was no wind and the night was superb: the water satin-smooth; the sky deep blue shading to a luminous rose near the horizon, streaked with wispy, purplish clouds; the gloomy, snow-streaked granite coast mirrored in an opalescent sea. Guillemots and murres, fleeing from our boats, pattered across the shimmering water.

Simata boiled more seal meat and a big pot of ink-black tea (the bailing can was also our chamber pot); we ate and drank and watched the rushing birds, and then we played cards with cookies as ante. Toward midnight, when it got very cold, Simata made a bed of caribou skins, blankets, and sleeping bags in the bow. She, several grandchildren, and I squeezed in and covered ourselves with a tarpaulin. Two piddling puppies squirmed in with us; it was crowded but cozy. Killiktee did not sleep. He stood in the stern, day and night and day, alert, observant, tireless.

It was he who spotted the beluga; the moist puffs of its breathing hung like plumes of frost in the rosy light of dawn. The lone beluga did not have a chance; the canoes fanned out like hunting killer whales. Each time the beluga surfaced to breathe, bullets forced it to dive until, exhausted, it surfaced long enough to be harpooned and killed. We hauled it onto an ice floe and saw that this had been a truly unfortunate whale. Months earlier it must have been imprisoned in a narrow lead and discovered by a polar bear, which had tried to kill it. Big pieces of skin and flesh had been ripped out of its body, and the entire melon — the fatty, bulbous frontal portion of the head — was torn away. The whale had somehow escaped, had miraculously survived the dreadful wounds that were now nearly healed, when misfortune led it into the path of even more deadly predators.

We reached the Savage Islands in the late afternoon of the second day, just as gray fog rolled over sea and land. Captain Thomas James, after whom James Bay is named, summarized Hudson Strait summer weather when he wrote in 1631: "The Weather for the most Part, a stinking Fog…"

We pulled the boats onto the ice foot of an island and set up camp near a creek 650 feet (200 m) inland. Here Inuit had lived and hunted for untold generations. Rust-eaten canisters and containers, perhaps obtained at the trade fairs or from nineteenth-century whalers, lay on the ground. Near our tents were the remains of seven Thule-culture houses. Whale bones, stones, and turf that had once formed rafters and walls filled the house

An inukshuk, *a distinctive, roughly man-shaped stone cairn, stands above the camp at the Savage Islands.*

The journey begins: provisions, people and tents are taken to the ice edge by snowmobile.

Arrival at the islands where the eiders nest.

Simeonie, Killiktee's grandson, with a teakettle full of eider eggs.

depressions, as well as broken tools and toys of bone and ivory, brown with age and encrusted with lichen. At two houses, great flat stone lintels were still in place, the doorways to houses used many centuries ago.

Noises and voices drifted through the fog; the creak and groan of tide-moved ice; the honking of Canada geese; the plaintive calling of red-throated loons; the lilting song of snow buntings; the haunting, mellow woodwind crooning of courting eider drakes.

Early next morning, the fog lifted. We climbed a hill topped by an *inukshuk*, an ancient, roughly man-shaped Inuit stone marker, and gazed across the sea dotted with dark granite islands bathed in the golden light of dawn.

Our boats full of pots, pails, zinc and plastic wash basins, and large wooden crates, we set out to raid the holms, the rocky islets that are the eiders' favorite nesting places. Men, women, and children stumbled across the algae-slippery coastal rocks of each islet, scrambled up the sheer ice foot, and then spread, screaming with glee, across the island as dozens of eiders, sometimes hundreds, rushed and clattered off their nests. Each nest was lined with a thick, soft layer of brownish gray-flecked eiderdown and contained, on the average, four large olive eggs. The Inuit took the eggs but left the down; traditionally they dressed in furs and had no use for down. Since it was early in the season, most ducks had just laid their eggs.

We rushed from island to island and collected eggs all day, and at night we feasted on them. The children, impatient, pricked many and sucked them dry. The adults preferred them hard-boiled. They made a filling meal; each egg, in volume, equals nearly two hen's eggs, and many Inuit ate six to ten at each meal. The albumen of the hard-boiled eider egg is a smooth, gleaming white, the yolk a vivid orange. The taste is rich and rather oily.

In a week we visited dozens of islets and amassed thousands of eggs. The Inuit also shot at least a hundred ducks and several seals. It seemed amazing that these yearly raids had not decimated the ducks. But they were made so early in the season that most of the robbed ducks probably laid another clutch of eggs.

Killiktee explained to me that in earlier days a taboo forbade the Inuit to camp on eider islands. They visited the islets and took the eggs, but they camped, as we did, only on the largest islands, where few ducks nest, thus avoiding prolonged disturbances in the breeding areas. The ducks, Killiktee said, seemed just as numerous now as sixty years ago when he had first visited the Savage Islands as a boy. Polar bears sometimes swim to the islands, kill all the ducks they can, and eat the eggs. One year, Killiktee said, while the Inuit were on holms, collecting eggs, a polar bear came to camp and robbed their stores. He ate at least a thousand eggs and crushed the rest, leaving a gooey mess upon the beach. Killiktee laughed, amused and without rancor. "Happy bear!" he said.

Less lucky was a gosling caught on an islet by one of the girls. She kept it in a Danish cookie tin and tried to make a pet of it. The fluffy yellow bird peeped pathetically and, inevitably, died after a few days. The girl cried, heartbroken, over her dead pet, and then she skinned it and ate it.

All crates were full of eggs, and ducks, seals, and whale meat filled the boats. The fog rolled in again and our boats traveled through a clammy, grayish, eerie emptiness. Killiktee led, the two other boats followed closely. Dark rocks appeared for moments and vanished into the gloomy gray; ice floes loomed up abruptly. Killiktee never hesitated. "How do you know where to go?" I asked. He smiled. "I know," he said. He had traveled along this coast a long lifetime; he had seen it, memorized it, knew every current, every shoal, every danger spot. He stood in the stern like a graven image and guided our boats through the weird gray void of the fog.

In the evening he veered into a bay, a good place, he said, to catch char on the rising tide. The men set nets, the women boiled pots of meat and tea, the children played. Killiktee, tired, lay down on the shore, and moments later he was sound asleep. A dark shape upon the dark, ice-carved granite, he seemed to meld with rock and land.

Back home at Kiijuak, all eggs were carefully examined. The cracked ones we ate soon. The others were placed in large crates and stored in a cool shady cleft among the rocks. They would last the people in our camp well into the winter.

In fall, an Inuk from Lake Harbour passed our camp and took me along to Aberdeen Bay where the people quarry the jade-green soapstone for their carvings. While he had tea and talked with Killiktee, I packed and carried my things to his boat. Killiktee came to the beach. We both felt awkward. Inuit traditionally joyfully greet visitors, but visitors leave in silence and alone with none to see

Elizabeth Arnajarnek feeds a pre-chewed morsel of caribou meat to her baby at a camp on the Barren Grounds in 1966.

Eider eggs are "candled" by peering through them against the bright sky.

These Baffin Island hunters are returning with meat and pelts from a caribou hunt.

them off. Their language has many words of welcome, but none for good-bye. Now Killiktee, ill at ease, shook my hand rather formally, and then his dark, deep-lined face lit up with a wonderfully warm smile. "Come back!" he said, went up the beach and continued to work on his outboard motor.

Two years later, I saw Killiktee once more. A nurse from a Montreal hospital called and asked: "Do you know a Mr. Killiktee?" For a moment my mind was blank, then the name clicked and I said yes. "He's in hospital," the nurse said. "You can visit him. He would be glad." She gave me the room number.

Maud and I went; she knew him from my stories and pictures. Simata was there. And Killiktee, looking wan and strangely frail in the austere white bed, dressed in one of those pathetic white hospital gowns that are open at the back. But his smile was as wonderfully warm as ever. We talked of this and that, and he wanted to see pictures from camp. I had asked one of the nurses, and she told me he had terminal cancer.

The next day we brought a projector and screen and showed pictures taken during the spring and summer I spent with him — the matchbox houses; Killiktee repairing his boat, helped by Eeshiak; cutting up the beluga on the ice floe; little Simeonie with a pail full of eider-duck eggs; the view from the top of the Savage Islands, the glowing sea at dawn, the dark granite islands where the eider ducks nest. There was a movement; I glanced at him and saw that tears ran down his face.

When he understood that he was dying, he insisted the doctors patch him up sufficiently to travel. "I go home," he said. He flew to Lake Harbour, then went by canoe to Kiijuak, and there he died on the land he loved.

Holding a caribou pelt in her tattooed hands, an old Inuk woman chews the last fat from the pelt before stretching it out to dry.

THE ALL-PURPOSE CARIBOU

Glorious it is to see
The caribou flocking down from the forests
And beginning
Their wandering to the north.
Timidly they watch
For the pitfalls of man.
Glorious it is to see
The great herds from the forests
Spreading out over plains of white.
Glorious to see.

— INUIT POEM
RECORDED BY KNUD RASMUSSEN IN THE EARLY 1920S

George Hakungak of Bathurst Inlet waits for the dog team to pick him up after a successful hunt.

A woman cleans a caribou skin while baking bannock over a seal-oil lamp.

Once they flowed like a living and life-giving tide across the tundra plains of the North. When the caribou came, an old Inuk told Knud Rasmussen in the 1920s, "the whole country is alive, and one can see neither the beginning of them nor the end — the whole earth seems to be moving."

Two animals were vital to human survival in the Arctic: seal and caribou. Seals provided food for humans and their sled dogs, strong, durable skins for boots and tents, and, above all, blubber that could be rendered into oil for the stone lamps of the Inuit, to cook their food, melt snow or ice into drinking water, dry their clothes, and warm their winter homes.

Caribou gave Inuit food and, through bones, hoofs, and antlers, a multitude of tools, toys, and weapons. Above all, from caribou skins Inuit women made the best Arctic clothing ever designed: light, durable, and so warm it made the wearer nearly impervious to any Arctic weather.

To kill caribou, Inuit used bows and arrows, lances, ambushes, traps, and a multitude of ingenious stratagems, many of them based on the hunters' knowledge of animal behavior and the quirks and weaknesses of their prey. Caribou are curious and myopic, and Inuit used these failings to get within shooting range — and that, before guns, was very close. The Inuit bow, made of pieces of driftwood, brittle and fragile, laboriously carved and pegged together, backed with plaited sinew cord to give it spring, and lashed with caribou or seal leather to give it strength, was a marvel of skill and ingenuity, but it was still a very weak weapon compared to bows of other regions where suitable wood was available. The longbow made of yew used by English archers to win the battle of Crécy in 1346 was deadly at 200 yards (180 m) and more. The Inuk bow, said Ekalun of Bathurst Inlet, who used it as a young hunter, killed only at thirty paces and less.

In 1967, I joined two Inuit hunters, Akpaleeapik and his brother

Akeeagok from Grise Fiord on Ellesmere Island, and their oldest sons on the last of the great polar-bear hunts made by Canadian Inuit. We left the village in April and returned in June, five people, two sleds and twenty-nine dogs, and never again in my life have I known such freedom. (The diaries I kept became the basis of my first book, *The Long Hunt.*) The rest of the world just ceased to be; time lost all meaning. We lived only for the here and now; it was a primal life, with primal joys — the endless travel through a pristine land; the great hardships of the trip; the satisfaction of being able to cope, endure, and overcome; and, although I do not hunt and never use a gun, the undeniable thrill of the hunt. And since we and our sled dogs were invariably famished after ten to twenty hours of travel every day, we looked forward with keen anticipation to our daily meal of seal or polar bear.

To hungry people every meal is a feast. A change of menu, however, is always welcome and when we crossed northern Devon Island in June and spotted caribou on a distant plain, Akeeagok took me along to hunt them. We sledged in a valley to the edge of the plain and then we played an ancient Inuit game of deception. We advanced across the white, open plain, pretending to be a caribou: Akeeagok with arms and gun held high was the antlered forepart; I, bent at right angles, my head in the small of his back, was the rear end of the caribou. The caribou, of course, spotted us instantly and were both curious and uneasy. Something, they realized, was not quite right. Whenever fear outweighed curiosity

This caribou-skin tent at Bathurst Inlet is warm but bulky.

Exhausted from carrying a heavy load of caribou meat, Jimmy Nakoolak sleeps on the tundra.

Koeenagnak, an Inuk of the Barrens, piles his plate with caribou meat. If he is very hungry, he will eat five to eight pounds (2 to 3.5 kg) of meat in a day.

and they seemed ready to flee, we turned in profile to them, showing the rough outline of a caribou, and Akeeagok grunted exactly like a caribou. Reassured, the caribou continued to stand and stare; once they even trotted toward us. When we were 30 yards (27 m) away, they finally panicked. But it was too late: Akeeagok shot and killed two animals. The others fled; he let them go. Both brothers were old-time hunters; they never killed more than we needed for food.

Another ruse Inuit hunters used also relied on the caribou's curiosity and shortsightedness. Two men walked past a herd. As they passed a boulder, one hid behind it and the other continued, waving, perhaps, a piece of white caribou belly skin to attract the curious animals. They followed him at a safe distance — and were shot by the hidden hunter.

In winter, Inuit cut pitfalls into drifts, covered them with thin sheets of hard Arctic snow, and baited them with urine, which caribou like for its saltiness. In spring and fall, they lay in wait with their kayaks where migrating caribou crossed rivers and lakes, and speared the swimming animals. And they built elaborate alignments of *inukshuit,* man-shaped cairns, on strategic ridges, which scared caribou herds toward hidden hunters. Women and children, crouched behind ridges and boulders, supplemented the line of stone men and, at a signal, rose and screamed. ("Hoo-hoo-hoo, they yelled, just like wolves," Ekalun recalled.)

Caribou meat was eaten fresh, or cut into strips and air-dried for future use. Fat fall caribou, often killed far from camp, were cut up and cached, food for the coming winter. Skins were made into clothing, bed robes, and tents.

Caribou sinew was the Inuit's thread. Plaited sinew cord was used to back the bow and give it elasticity and spring. It was used as fishing lines, and as guy lines for the tent. Depilated caribou skin was made into containers and packsacks, and covered the kayaks of inland Inuit. Toggles for dog-team harnesses were carved of caribou bone, as were the prongs of leisters (where musk-ox horn was not available), spear blades and arrowheads, and a diabolically ingenious wolf killer. Sharpened splinters of caribou shin bone were set into ice and covered with blood and fat. When a wolf came along and licked the blood, it lacerated its tongue on the frozen-in bone knife and, excited by the taste of fresh blood, licked and bled and licked and bled until it died; its skin was used for clothing.

Caribou antlers were boiled and immersed in hot water and then straightened with a *qatersiorfik,* a big bone or palmate piece of antler into which a large hole had been worked. (Identical implements were made by reindeer hunters of the Aurignacian and Magdalenian periods in Europe, 15,000 to 30,000 years ago. Under the delusion that these were symbols of ancient authority, archaeologists have given them the grandiloquent name *bâtons de commandement.*) Straightened antler sections were scarfed, glued (with caribou blood), pegged (with pegs of caribou bone), and lashed (with strips of moist caribou skin), and made into spear shafts, tent poles, leister handles, and sled sections.

All was used, nothing was wasted. What humans did not eat, their sled dogs did. Caribou provided Inuit with food, clothing, shelter, and many tools and weapons. It was essential to life and lived in their legends and myths. The newborn Inuit baby was wiped clean with a piece of caribou fur, and when an Inuk died his shroud was made of caribou skins.

Caribou were in their thoughts and caribou marched through their dreams. In spring at Bathurst Inlet, as we waited for caribou to come to our far-northern coast, Ekalun on the sleeping platform next to me often mumbled in his sleep, and it was "*tuktu*," always "*tuktu*," endless herds of caribou, migrating through the sleeping mind of the old hunter.

ARCTIC CLOTHING: COMFORT IN A COLD CLIMATE

Humans originated in a warm climate, probably in Africa. Nature did not design them for cold weather. Naked humans today are comfortable at an ambient air temperature of about 75°F (24°C). When the air temperature is low enough to sap body heat faster than it can be generated, the body's core temperature is lowered and we are immediately in grave trouble. Our normal body temperature is 98.6°F (37°C). At 91°F (33°C), our thermoregulatory system begins to falter.

The winter fur of an arctic fox provides such perfect insulation that even at forty below and in windy conditions he does not have to increase his metabolic rate. He rolls into a ball, tucks his nose beneath his bushy tail, and sleeps, as blissfully warm as a human in the shade of a palm tree in the tropics. A naked human exposed to a temperature of forty below and winds of 30 miles (48 km) per hour — conditions common in the Arctic — dies in about fifteen minutes. But rather than travel the slow road of evolution and produce a densely furred, cold-resistant human strain, man took the cultural shortcut of skinning the cold-adapted fox and wearing its fur.

Fox fur is wonderfully warm, but the hairs are soft and the fur mats easily. Musk-ox fur is even warmer, but very heavy. Parkas made of bird skins, of eider ducks on the Belcher Islands and dovekie skins in Greenland, are light and warm, but fragile. Seal skins are strong, but not warm. By far the best fur for Arctic clothing, virtually the *sine qua non* of Inuit survival in the Arctic, is that of the caribou.

Caribou hairs are club shaped, thicker at the tips than at their

The rear slit in the fur suit of Inuit toddlers closes when they stand and opens when they stoop.

When the caribou died out on the Belcher Islands in Hudson Bay, the Inuit made parkas of eider duck skins.

base, so that they trap body warmth in tiny air spaces near the skin, and each hair is filled with air cells. The fur is short, but very warm; the skin is light, but very strong.

The Inuit make every effort to kill caribou for winter clothing (and for food) in August and early September, when the fur is of optimum quality. Seven skins were required to dress a man, six a woman, and four a child. The skins were carefully cleaned of meat and fat, and laid hair-down upon pebbly ground to dry as quickly as possible. Once dry, the skins were scraped with several different types of bone or stone scrapers — a hard and tedious task shared by men and women — until they were as soft as chamois leather.

An experienced Inuit seamstress could take the measure of her man at a glance, cut the required patterns from the skins with her *ulu*, the half-moon-shaped woman's knife, then sew the pieces together with closely spaced, overcast stitches. Dried caribou sinew was her thread, ideal because it is very strong and molds itself to leather but does not tear it. (Inuit women now often use waxed dental floss as a sinew substitute.) Her thimble was made of musk-ox horn or of depilated bearded-seal leather; her needle of the hard wing bone of gull or goose, or a polished splinter of caribou bone.

A complete winter outfit consisted of an inner parka worn with the hair against the body, an outer parka worn fur-out, inner and outer pants worn in the same manner, fur stockings, boots, and mittens. Wolverine fur (or that of wolf or dog) was used for the ruff of the loose-fitting parka hood because hoarfrost formed by breath could easily be brushed from it. Stockings were made of caribou fur or the down-soft fur of Arctic hare; the boot sole from extremely strong and stiff bearded-seal leather; the upper portion of the boot of ringed-seal leather. A layer of dried grass, usually replaced each day, was put into the boot to form an insole that provided extra insulation and absorbed moisture. Mittens were made of caribou skin, often with a palm inset of durable seal leather.

The entire outfit weighed just over 10 pounds (4.5 kg). It was loose and airy enough not to cause sweating, yet warm enough to enable a hunter, as Knud Rasmussen observed, to stand "motionless as a statue" above a seal's breathing hole "in a storm and in a temperature of about −50°C [−58°F]." One man, Rasmussen reported, stood thus for two days and two nights, tired but warm in his superlative clothing. "When an Eskimo is well dressed," said the explorer Vilhjalmur Stefansson, "his two layers of fur clothing imprison the body heat so effectively that the air in actual contact with the skin is always at the temperature of a tropical summer."

Inuit, well dressed, did not fear the Arctic cold, and they did not necessarily find other countries and climates more genial and alluring. Kallihiruas, a young Polar Inuk from northwest Greenland, was taken to England by an 1851 Arctic expedition. He lived for four years in Canterbury and, dressed in European clothes, was pitifully cold. In 1855, he wrote a plaintive letter to an English friend: "I been in England long time, none very well. Very bad weather… I very sorry, very bad weather dreadful. Country very different. Another day cold. Another day wet. I miserable…" (The coldest winter I ever spent was in London, England. I had "rooms" [one room!] at a so-called good address, a lovely Edwardian house near Hampstead Heath, with ceilings that were 12 feet [4 m] high, windows of nearly equal height that, even closed, let so much icy air in that the curtains billowed, and a miniature gas heater that produced feeble warmth to a distance of about 3 feet [1 m] and ate sixpences at half-hour intervals. I saw a lot of plays that winter; it was warmer and cheaper than feeding coins into that greedy heater meter.)

To give total protection against the killing Arctic cold, Inuit clothes had to be perfectly dry or they lost their insulating quality. At the entrance to each winter home stood an *anowtaq*, a snow beater of bone or wood, with which Inuit brushed and beat all snow from their clothes before entering. The outer layers of clothes were left in a cold, dry anteroom igloo, or chamber, and socks, boots, and mittens were carefully dried each night on a webbed drying rack suspended above a seal-oil lamp.

The inferiority of my winter clothing and the superiority of Inuit clothing was painfully impressed upon me during one of my first lengthy Arctic trips. In 1966, I went to the village of Igloolik, on northwestern Hudson Bay, to photograph a spring festival. There I met Pewatook, an Inuk from a far-away camp, who agreed to take me home. He looked askance at my army surplus winter outfit, but was too polite to say anything.

It was drifting so hard the day we traveled by dog team the 65 miles (104 km) to his camp on Jens Munk Island in northern Foxe Basin that I could barely see the lead dog. Yet Pewatook guided his team unerringly through the whirling snow, traversing a maze of pressure ridges, to arrive fifteen hours later at the door of his house, a small white mound in an endless expanse of white.

Half a dozen steps, screened by a porch of snow blocks, led to a first door. This opened into a large anteroom igloo, where the bulky fur clothing was stored, cold and dry, on one side, while the other side was piled high with cut-up carcasses of caribou, seal, and walrus. The igloo was roofed with blocks of fresh-water ice, and was suffused on bright days by a beautiful blue-green light. From the igloo a second door led into a narrow, upward-sloping passage, a cold trap, and a third door opened into the spacious living quarters of two families.

This portion of the house consisted of a wooden shell, covered from the outside with a thick layer of snow blocks, and from the inside with cardboard. For added insulation, magazine pages had been glued onto the cardboard with flour paste, including pages

A Polar Inuit woman chews a sealskin boot sole to make it supple for sewing

The day is relatively warm (-6° F /-20° C), so Pewatook wears only his inner caribou-skin parka.

Through energetic scraping, caribou skins are made as soft as chamois leather.

from *Playboy.* Four large soapstone *kudlit* (seal-oil lamps) burned day and night and kept the place quite warm.

At the far end of the room was the sleeping platform covered with caribou furs. The right-hand corner (seen from the door) was the realm of Tatigat, Pewatook's wife. There she kept her possessions, tended her kudlit, sewed clothes, and cooked meals. During rare idle hours, she and Pewatook sat close together, a large sheet of plywood on their outstretched legs and upon it the pieces of a huge jigsaw puzzle, one of those monochromatic landscape miseries, all soft blues and greens, that are so exceedingly hard to assemble. Even allowing for the fact that they had probably done the puzzle many times, their visual acuity in spotting matching pieces was astounding.

The left-hand corner of the sleeping platform belonged to their son Malliki; his wife, Erkarasa; and their three children, Kattanak, her brother Attaguatiak, and the baby Panipak. For me they made a fur bed in the opposite corner of the house and gave me a stand with a large kudlik. This crescent-shaped lamp of ancient design was carved of soapstone. The basin was filled with seal oil; the wick, along the straight edge of the lamp, was made of dried moss mixed with the bolls of arctic cottongrass.

When well trimmed, the lamp burned with an even, 2-inch (5-cm)-high yellow flame along its 2-foot (60-cm) length, that gave off some light and a considerable amount of warmth. When the flame burned unevenly, peaks flared and sooted. One is then supposed to tamp the wick with the *tarkut*, the small hammer-shaped stone lamp trimmer. I couldn't get it right; my flame looked like a fever graph. Either I put the flame out altogether, or it flared evilly and sent tiny tendrils of soot into the air.

Seven-year-old Kattanak watched this for a while, then came over and, with a few deft taps of the tarkut, adjusted my wick to perfection. From then on she became the guardian of my lamp and, to some extent, of me as well. Since I was evidently incompetent, she somehow felt it her duty to look after me: she checked my boots, dried my socks, and trimmed my lamp with serious-eyed efficiency.

Every morning, fair weather or foul (mostly foul!), Pewatook readied the great sled to make the two-hour trip to the floe edge. The sled was turned upside down, and its runners, shod with pieces from the jawbone of a bowhead whale Pewatook killed in 1965, were covered with water, which instantly froze into a smooth film of ice, so that the sled glided nearly frictionless over snow and ice. The dogs, yelping with eager excitement, were harnessed. The last equipment was pushed under the sled's lashings, and seconds later we were off in a cloud of silvery snow.

It was a rough trip. We crossed many pressure ridges, high jumbles of upturned ice blocks, and Pewatook guided the heavy sled, jumping on and off with cat-like agility despite his sixty years and his voluminous fur clothing. Near the last pressure ridge we picked up his umiak, really a plywood punt, 6 feet (180 cm) long and 2 feet (60 cm) wide, nailed together and covered with sealskins. This we lashed onto the sled, and from then on we rode in the boat on the sled, a wise precaution since a dip at forty below is bound to result in death from exposure.

On calm, cold nights, the floe edge "grew" out into the sea for a mile or more. While slowly freezing sea ice has a salinity of about two parts per mill, fast-frozen sea ice may have a salinity of twenty parts per mill. Increased salinity gives sea ice greater tensile strength; it bends alarmingly but (one hopes) does not break.

This newly formed sea ice looks matte gray from a distance. It is covered by long ice crystals, all standing erect and glittering in the sun like myriad frosty leaves. The ice looked uniform, but Pewatook's trained eye could spot weak areas from a distance. A call to the dogs, and we neatly skirted the dangerous region. It did not always work this way. Once we had waited in vain for seals for many hours. We left to look for a better spot; the dogs were cold

Kattanak, the little guardian of my seal-oil lamp, is plastered with snow after a long trip in a storm.

and eager to run. They streaked across the smooth ice, so thin (2 or 3 inches [5 or 7 cm]!) one could feel it bend underneath the weight of the sled. Suddenly Pewatook saw a particularly weak wedge, some 30 yards (27 m) wide, and called to the dogs. But they were in full gallop and kept on going. They yelped with fear when the film of rubber-like ice buckled under their weight, but it held, the dogs kept running, and the momentum carried the sled across as well. When I looked back, black water was bubbling up in our tracks.

We spent about twelve hours every day at the floe edge. In the severe cold, it seemed a sinister place. At forty below, the sea water is about sixty-eight degrees warmer than the surrounding air and it literally steams. Dark gray vapor hung like a perpetual pall above the water. The ice was thin and dangerous. It was moist and intensely cold. Pewatook, in full fur regalia, was indifferent to the cold: within his furs he was toasty warm. He stood hour after hour near the open water and scratched the ice with his harpoon shaft. The grating noise travels far in water and often attracts curious seals.

In the meantime, I suffered. Pewatook knew that my store-bought clothing — drill parka and quilted pants — was just adequate to protect me from serious damage. Like all old-time Inuit with whom I have ever lived, he felt a great sense of responsibility for me, since I had entrusted myself to his care, and he made sure that I did not freeze to death or drown. That with my inadequate clothing I would be miserably cold, he knew too, but that was my choice and my problem. While he stood motionless as a statue and waited for seals, I trotted back and forth, and froze and suffered.

When he shot a seal, we unleashed the punt and he paddled out into the ominous gray, swirling fog to retrieve it. And then he waited for more seals to appear, with the infinite patience of the true hunter. It was forty below, and blowing. In his caribou-skin clothing he was as warm as a tourist on a Florida beach, while my very soul congealed and tinkled somewhere in my body.

Each evening, just when the cold seemed to become unbearable, Pewatook would turn to me and ask, "*Ikee*? (Are you cold?)," smile broadly about my shivery "Yes!," load the sled, and off we sped for home and the blessed warmth of the camp.

With great patience and skill, Pewatook and Tatigat assemble a huge jigsaw puzzle.

> *Our gloves are stiff with the frozen blood,*
> *Our furs with the drifted snow,*
> *As we come home with the seal — the seal!*
> *In from the edge of the floe.*
>
> — RUDYARD KIPLING, "ANGUTIVAUN TAINA,"
> FROM *THE SECOND JUNGLE BOOK*

EKALUN'S CAMP

Ekalun's winter tent, my home at Bathurst Inlet.

SHIP-BORNE EUROPEAN EXPLORERS POKED AND PENETRATED THE North American Arctic from east and west. The central portion, the "region of inaccessibility" as it was called, was hard to reach by ship from either direction and remained for a long time unexplored and unknown.

To reach this *terra incognita* and find, if possible, the missing central portion of the Northwest Passage, John Franklin and a large crew of English explorers, French-Canadian voyageurs, and Copper Indians descended the Coppermine River in 1821, followed the Arctic coast as far east as Turnagain Point on Kent Peninsula, then raced winter back through Bathurst Inlet, passing close to the site of Ekalun's future camp, and ascended the Hood River. Winter nearly won: by the time survivors reached Fort Providence in December, half the expedition members had died. They had seen many signs of Inuit, but had not met the people.

In 1902, the English explorer David T. Hanbury crossed the mouth of Bathurst Inlet. He met a few Inuit, whom he found "most friendly."

The Natives were less friendly in 1912, when the American explorers Radford and Street whipped an Inuk who was unwilling to be their guide because his wife was sick. Considering these men mad and dangerous, the Inuit stabbed them to death.

Inspector Francis H. French of the Royal North-West Mounted Police (later called the Royal Canadian Mounted Police) set out from Hudson Bay to investigate the fate of the missing explorers. He left by dog team in the fall of 1916, traveled overland and reached Bathurst Inlet in 1917, carried out his investigations, and returned to Baker Lake, west of Hudson Bay, in 1918, having completed a dog-team "patrol" of more than 5,000 miles (8000 km). He spoke to many Inuit, including the men who killed the explorers, but he made no arrests because, he stated in his report, "I would judge that they [the Inuit] only acted in self-defence and to protect themselves, as the only law they know is self-protection."

Bathurst Inlet was finally thoroughly explored by the 1913–18 Stefansson–Anderson Canadian Arctic expedition. In the summer of 1915, they stopped at an Inuit fishing camp not far from the mouth of the Hood River. These were the first whites this group of Inuit had ever seen, and they stood on shore and stared at them, strange, nearly mythic beings from another world with a boat that was filled with treasures: articles made of metal. Among them was a fur-clad, ten-year-old boy named Ekalun. Fifty-four years later, his

Ekalun, well into his sixties, removes white hairs with tweezers.

most vivid memory of that encounter was that he had been filled with a mixture of amazement and avarice. "They looked strange," he recalled. "They had lots of hair on their faces. They talked strange. And they had so many wonderful things." He laughed. "I wanted to steal everything. We did not know how we could buy things then. We just kept hoping the white men would give us some of their things."

If the Natives had trouble understanding the world of the wealthy strangers, the latter, in turn, could not comprehend the total independence of Inuit, to whom the very concept of service, of master and man, was alien. To further their exploration work they had hoped to obtain "service from the local aborigines," but that came to nothing because the Natives had "no idea of working for anyone."

The life of the people then was ruled by the seasons. During the dark period in late December and early January, Ekalun said, "We danced and sang and told stories," living off fish and meat cached the previous fall. In winter and spring, they hunted seals at agloos, their breathing holes. In late spring and summer, many traveled far inland to hunt caribou. In autumn, they returned to the coast to spear char with leisters and to hunt fat fall caribou for meat and skins for winter clothing. "We worked hard then," said Ekalun. "We traveled much. If one was lucky, one had lots to eat. If one had no luck, one was hungry. Often one was hungry. But then came again good times. And the people were happy and danced."

In 1923, the people of this region were visited by Knud Rasmussen during his epic three-year dog-team trip from Thule in northwest Greenland to Alaska and Siberia. He found them "inflammable" and "very temperamental," but also noted that "as poets they were perhaps the most gifted and inspired Eskimos I have ever fallen in with."

An exuberant Ekalun beats a large drum and sings an ancient song of his people.

Missionaries came to Bathurst Inlet, and Ekalun, until then a "pagan," was baptized and received a Christian name, Patrick, and his young wife, Kongyona, became Rosie Kongyona. About that time his first son was born, and Ekalun, who until then had hunted with bow and arrow, acquired his first gun.

The 1950s and 1960s brought enormous changes to the North. Most Inuit left the land and moved into the nascent towns and villages. But the people of Bathurst Inlet remained remote and nearly untouched, and in the winter of 1969 I left again my city and family life and went north to join them. The dry Arctic snow creaked and groaned underneath the runners of our heavy sled. "*Kayornaktuk*! (It is cold!)," said Joseph Tikhek. "It will be good to get home." We had traveled for eight days by dog team from Cambridge Bay on Victoria Island across wind-swept Dease Strait and over the rolling, rock-strewn icy plains of Kent Peninsula. Now we were nearing our goal, the winter camp of Joseph's family at Arctic Sound, on the west coast of Bathurst Inlet.

I snuggled deeper into my heavy parka to escape the cutting wind, and worried about my welcome. There had been no chance to warn the people at this remote camp of my arrival. I hoped to stay at least six months and I knew, after all, exactly what my reaction would be if a Chinese anthropologist studying Canadians turned up at our Montreal house one day and said: "Hi, folks! You mind if I live with you for half a year?" and proceeded to set up his cot in our bedroom.

It was dark now. In the distance a husky howled dolefully. A faint orange light glimmered through the gloom. Our dogs, happy to be home, broke into a wild gallop. Fur-clad shapes rushed out to greet us. "My mother will take care of the dogs," Joseph said. "Come into my father's house."

I followed him through a narrow passage of snow blocks into a large, double-layered tent. Children were sleeping on the raised, fur-covered snow platform at the rear. Moses Panegyuk, Joseph's father, smiled his welcome. "Tea is nearly ready," he said. We talked of the trip. Others crowded into the tent. Not by a word, not by a gesture did anyone betray the slightest surprise or puzzlement at my unexpected presence. It would have been impolite. The stranger must be made welcome, not plied with questions.

A sleepy, round face peeked out from underneath the furs on the sleeping platform and stared at me in wide-eyed wonder. "Aiee, *Kabloona*! (A white man!)" little Oched squealed and hid in fright, and we laughed and chatted, and drank the sweet, scalding hot tea, squatting on the low snow benches at the side of the tent. It was good to be home.

"You will live with my grandfather," said Joseph, who had earlier slipped out of the tent. We walked through the crystal-clear, star-glittering night to the far tent of this four-tent community. Ekalun,

In the spring, caribou meat is the main food in camp. This child is sucking marrow out of a bone.

his grandfather, was already in bed. With his narrow, powerful face, aquiline nose and shaved head, except for a tuft of hair above his brow, he looked like a haughty Indian chieftain. The face was a mirror of the man, strong and self-reliant, fearless and free. There was kindness in that face, but also a hint of ruthlessness, and traces of that sardonic, mordant wit of which I would so often be the butt during the coming months. Rosie Kongyona, small and active, bustled busily over the pressure stove, the tattoo lines on her dark brow bunched into a concentrated frown, as she tried to hurry the tea along.

"Ekalun," I said, "I have come for a long time. Is it all right?"

He waved his hand over the snow platform. "This is your home," he said simply. And my home it was for the next six months.

It was winter and our food came from the frozen sea. Every morning the long sleds were readied, the runners covered with water, which instantly froze into a polished glaze, the dogs harnessed, and our long canine caravan rushed off to the sealing grounds, 15 miles (24 km) to the north.

Each ringed seal has from four to a dozen or more breathing holes, called agloos by the Inuit. The seal scrapes and gnaws these holes as soon as ice forms in fall and keeps them open in the fast-thickening ice as vital vents to the air above. Snow covers the agloos, and the Inuit have to rely on their dogs to find them. We parked the teams near an island, each man took two dogs on a long leash, grabbed his harpoon, and trotted after the dogs, zig-zagging over the wind-fluted snow.

Once the dogs found an agloo, the hunter searched for nearby breathing holes, cut the snow away to spook the seal, and finally chose one hole. He inserted a long thin sliver of wood, the *idlak*, into the agloo, a colored tassel attached to its top. When the seal comes up to breathe, the indicator stick jiggles and the hunter

Harpoon at the ready, a hunter waits for a seal to surface in its breathing hole.

plunges his harpoon through the snow into the seal. It was an ancient hunt, unchanged for thousands of years, and it required endless patience and total concentration.

I followed Moses. He ran quickly after his dogs as they sniffed around here and there, until I was soaked in sweat. Finally he found a promising agloo, inserted the idlak, spread a piece of thick caribou fur on the snow to muffle even the slightest noise from his feet, and froze into immobility, bent over like a three-quarter-closed jacknife, his eyes riveted to the tiny colored tassel, his harpoon at the ready. I watched him from a distance. An hour passed and two. Moses did not move. The bitter cold crept through my clothes. I walked to get warm. In the distance dark figures stood motionless over other agloos: Ekalun; his sons, George Hakungak and John Akana; and Joseph Kaneak, his son-in-law.

I looked at my watch. Four hours. Moses had not budged. His whole being seemed concentrated upon that tiny dot of color on the head of his idlak. Suddenly he straightened, lifted his harpoon, and drove it down in one smooth, immensely powerful stroke. Holding the rawhide harpoon line with one hand, he cut away snow and ice with his long snow knife to haul the seal out of the hole. And then he found another agloo and resumed his patient vigil.

The day passed. The men did not stir. A three-quarter moon rose above the bluish haze of dusk. I walked to the island and

Rosie Kongyona, Ekalun's wife, took good care of me for half a year.

Rosie Kongyona spoons porridge into her grandson Oched.

climbed a hill, and the Earth was "without form, and void"; it was
our world on the day of creation, vast and silent, oppressively
lonely, and apparently without life.

At last they gave up. Moses had his seal. The others had nothing
after waiting, statue-still, for fifteen hours. Ekalun lost a seal. After
waiting all day, the seal did come, but Ekalun's harpoon touched a
small piece of ice and was deflected from its true aim. "*Mamiena.*
(It is not good.)" was Ekalun's only comment.

It was forty below. The dogs were cold and eager to run. Our
dog teams and sleds, dark dots and dashes, rushed through the
diaphanous blue of the Arctic night. In this strangely phantasmagoric
world of shifting shapes and shadows, this world without depth
and distance, legends and lore of the Inuit assume new meaning.
Their fears and ghosts and specters become real and somehow
right, for these spirits were born in the blue-gray gloom of the
Arctic night. On Moses's sled was the dead seal, our life-giving
food.

At home we feasted. Ella Tonakahok, Moses's wife, quickly cut
up and boiled the seal, and soon a huge platter of steaming meat,
blubber, and intestines lay in the center of the tent. Ella stirred a
bucket of blood into the seal broth, so we could have blood soup
after the main course.

Our camp was really one big family. We ate from tent to tent.
"*Tee-toi-té.* (Tea's up!)" Rosie called early in the morning, and the
whole community crowded into our tent for tea and chunks of raw
caribou meat and the dry, white, tallow-like back fat cached after
the previous year's fall hunt. Then we all trooped over to Ella's for a
second breakfast, to Hakungak's for a third, and to Kaneak's for a
fourth. Proud the hunter, and happy and busy his wife, who had
the most meat to offer, or who had special delicacies: vitamin-rich
liver; strips of rubbery, sweetish intestine; and seal stomachs full of

*A late-winter storm sweeps
across Ekalun's camp.*

greenish, half-digested shrimps that tasted like lobster paste.

Ekalun was head of this large family. Language is revealing: Inuit have no term for chief or boss or master. They were a society of equals. Ekalun had authority, yet he never obviously wielded it. Ours was a tight and generally harmonious community made up of very independent and individualistic people. All adults were busy with self-assigned tasks; the children slept, played, or helped. All food was shared, as was tobacco. After one of our first meals at Kaneak's, I searched for my pipe. Ekalun pushed Kaneak's tobacco can over. "Smoke," he said; then, with a grin, he added: "We are not like people in the south who, as they tell me, like to keep things for themselves. What we have, we share."

Some days there was little to share. Blinding blizzards imprisoned us in our tents. The men carved, repaired hunting gear, or slept. The women scraped caribou skins and sewed them into warm and beautiful garments, decorated with intricate, inlaid patterns of light- and dark-haired caribou skin, and tassels of wolverine fur; the skin side stained red with crushed litharge, a rock pigment; the hood an immense ruff of wolf fur. To make a simple suit might have taken a few days. To make it so beautiful took weeks.

Ekalun and Rosie sang while they worked, long chant-like ballads of former days. Both were fussy about their appearance. Ekalun spent hours each week removing facial hairs with tweezers. "You should shave, Kabloo," he said, looking disapprovingly at my sprouting beard. "You look like a musk-ox!" Then Rosie laid her head in his lap, and with infinite patience he pulled out every white hair. And Rosie was a great-grandmother!

I fitted easily into this community. As a nonhunting male, I was an anomaly to them, but since I was harmless, happily ate their food, and made no special demands, they accepted me with easy nonchalance. As far as they were concerned, I was odd and useless but basically not a problem. I usually left each morning with the men and walked for hours while they hunted. Or I stayed in camp and watched the women work, or photographed the children. It was a quietly harmonious life, and suddenly it ended.

A bad blizzard locked us in for days. When I awoke on the fifth day, the weather was glorious, and Rosie and Ekalun were busily bustling in and out of the tent. "Where are you going?" I asked. To a remote island, he said, to get soapstone of a special color. I knew of the island. There were ancient Inuit houses upon it, a soapstone quarry of great antiquity, and beaches where people used to collect chunks of native copper. I very much wanted to see that island and, above all, I wanted to travel. "I'm coming along," I said. "I'll be ready right away." Ekalun stopped. "It is not good," he said. "The dogs are not strong. The others will give you food." I should have heeded his veiled rejection. But I insisted; since I was a paying boarder, I felt I had a right to come along. Ekalun demurred, mumbled something about the weather not being good, unharnessed the dogs, unloaded the sled, then went into the tent and worked on a carving. The trip, evidently, was off. Later I met Joseph Tikhek. "The old man is very angry with you," he said, and that was the last thing anyone said to me. I simply ceased to be.

At first I did not take it seriously. *Quel vecchio maledivami!* I noted flippantly in my diary, but I quickly learned that this curse, like the one in *Rigoletto*, was nothing to joke about. The adults ignored me, the children shunned me, the sled dogs snarled at me.

I do not mind being alone, I have often spent weeks alone on islands off Alaska, observing and photographing seals and birds. On good days I'm busy; on bad days I walk; on truly miserable days I lie in my tent and read those books I always meant to read but somehow never found the time for.

But this was ostracism, the penultimate punishment of a people who have neither laws nor law enforcement (the ultimate — and final — punishment is death). By my impetuous demand to be taken along, I had broken a basic rule of their society: one does not impose one's will upon another person, thereby limiting his freedom; one does not interfere with other people's plans and actions. For this I was being punished. Where before there had been pleasant acceptance and I was a part of the camp, there was now hostile rejection. I no longer belonged. I still shared their food but nothing else.

Neuroses are fantastic flowers; if you keep a detailed diary, you can watch them grow and blossom. Within a week mine were in full bloom. I sulked. I nurtured small-boy grievances and dreamed of revenge: "I'll walk out and, if it kills me, then they'll be sorry!" I went for endless walks to escape the silent hostility of camp.

George Hakungak takes careful aim at a distant caribou

A tent at night on an Arctic bay.

Jessie and George Hakungak and their child Karetak travel across the tundra in the summer of 1969. Pack dogs carry part of their load.

Ekalun was very shrewd. He wanted me punished but he did not want a nut in camp, nor did he want me wandering off into the Arctic sunset, a not-uncommon end of northern neurotics. After eight days, he must have felt that this was enough and that I should have learned my lesson.

I returned late from one of my sulky marathon walks, glum and famished. Rosie had just called: "Seal's ready!" and all were in her tent. I squeezed in and squatted near the door. The quiet of our meal, so pleasantly relaxed before, now seemed ominously tense and brooding. I ate quickly, nervously. It gave me something to do.

Suddenly Ekalun looked up and smiled. "You walk all day alone, like *amarok*, the wolf. And now you eat just like a wolf." I recognized that tone of voice. It was the gentle banter of before. I laughed and then the others laughed, and our common laughter lifted the icy cloud from me and it vanished in a wave of friendly warmth. I once again belonged. I was deeply happy and content, and henceforth took the greatest care to curb my assertiveness so I would not offend again. Thus, slowly, sometimes painfully, by prod and praise, and various sanctions and rewards, they modified my behavior to conform more closely to their culturally accepted norms. It works with children (and with dogs), and it worked with me.

In May, the weather turned mild and muggy. Agloo hunting was finished. Our thoughts turned southward, to the land. It, now, must give us food. The caribou must come, on their annual migration from the taiga, the northern forest belt, over the vastness of the Barren Ground tundra, to the Arctic Sea.

Each day Ekalun and his sons climbed the mountain behind our camp to scan the land and sea patiently with their telescopes. And each day they came down from the mountain and shrugged. "*Tuktu nauk.* (No caribou.)" Our stores of seal meat and blubber dwindled

Cleaned sealskins are pegged out to dry.

rapidly. The children fished for tomcod at fissures in the ice.

Rosie went inland, with a big bag of traps, to the sandy ridges where perky ground squirrels were emerging from their long winter's sleep to bask in the spring sun. She walked fast, her small, work-worn body bent forward, set a series of traps and rushed off to the next *siksik* (squirrel) colony, while I trotted behind through the mushy spring snow, out of breath and oozing sweat. At night, the squirrels boiled in a big pot, pink little paws poking pathetically out of the bubbling broth. They tasted like chicken. Squirrels and the little fish the children brought home were now our main food.

Ekalun's automatic Swiss watch had stopped. "Here, Kabloo, you fix it," he said. I recoiled at the idea, and Ekalun laughed derisively. "I thought white men were supposed to be so clever," he gibed and began to take it apart. The tools he lacked he made, a few out of Rosie's darning needles. He remembered the days when the only tools his people had were of stone, bone, horn, and native copper. He had shown me how to make a stone adze, and it was similar to the ones I had seen in Paris's Musée de l'Homme made by Magdalenian hunters 20,000 years ago. Now he nonchalantly took the watch apart. Before evening he had assembled the watch again — and it worked.

Our camp was nearly out of food; one cannot live long on lean spring squirrels and small fish. The families dispersed, traveling far inland to intercept the vanguard of migrating caribou. The talk in camp was of tuktu — caribou — always tuktu, the quail and manna of the Barrens.

Ekalun remained. He was carving a chess set: the board superbly inlaid with polished stones of many colors; the rooks were igloos, the knights polar bears, the bishops dogs, the pawns a little army of obese owls. King and queen were Inuit in full fur regalia. "My wife and I," he said, and smiled. The carved stone king did, in fact, look like Ekalun. It would take weeks to finish the set. And food? "The caribou will come," he said confidently.

I left with George Hakungak; his beautiful wife, Jessie; their two small children; and John Akana, George's bachelor brother. The dogs pulled eagerly, although they had fallen upon hard times. We only had a bit of blubber along, and old caribou skins for roughage.

We snaked our way up the great Hood River valley. After winter's long dormancy, the tundra throbbed with resurrection, with renewal, with life. Elegant horned larks spiraled toward the sky until they were but specks in the blue, then drifted gently downward on set wings, filling the air with their jubilant, lilting song. Ptarmigan flew up, their plumage piebald like the land, part wintry white, part summer's brown. From its nest of sticks and dry grasses on a ledge above the ice-bound river, a rough-legged hawk rose to circle high above us with wild and urgent cries. The day was warm and brilliant, the dogs ran fast, the long sled slid silently through the wet

The great, uncluttered world beyond camp is the children's playground.

snow. We joked and laughed. It was wonderful to be alive.

That night the storm struck. Wind-driven snow wreathed the mountains like smoke. It shrieked around our small traveling tent and whistled eerily in the taut guy ropes. Jessie washed diapers. John carved. George played with the baby. While the storm raged, life went on quietly and harmoniously within the walls of our little tent.

It was night when the storm faltered. Dark clouds still scudded across the sky; the land and a nearby frozen lake lay in an ominous blue-gray El Greco light. And then the caribou came, and in their wake the wolves.

Far out on the lake ice, dark and phantom-like, the herd stood. The men harnessed the huskies and drove fast, right into the herd, the dogs frenzied with excitement, the sled slewing wildly, the caribou scattering, stopping, galloping frantically back and forth, fear forcing them to flee, the herd instinct bunching them. George and John stopped and shot, raced on and shot again, then turned the dogs loose to pull down wounded caribou.

We camped for days to feed the famished, emaciated dogs, to eat huge meals ourselves, our first in weeks, and then, the sled loaded high with caribou meat, we walked the 100 miles (160 km) back to camp. Thaw and rain had ravaged the snow; meltwater rushed to the rivers. The broad, tussocky meadows were bare and brown, and George and John harnessed themselves to the sled to help the panting huskies.

Before breakup, the planes arrived. The doctor from Cambridge Bay on medical inspection found us well, but left us germs, and soon we all came down with colds. The area administrator arrived to buy the men's stock of carvings, the fur clothes the women had made for sale, and one of our caribou-skin tents for a museum in the United States.

On the first good day, we left for Baychimo at the northeast coast of Bathurst Inlet to buy supplies at the lonely Hudson's Bay Company store. It then served the eighty-nine people of Bathurst Inlet, who lived in eleven widely scattered camps in a region as large as Belgium.

People from other camps had preceded us, or arrived during the day. Ekalun, one of the best carvers of the area, had the most money. With a fine sense of drama, he waited until the store was crowded. Every inch the grand seigneur, he strode in and handed Jimmy Stevenson, the manager, his checks. Then he started buying, and the Queen shopping at Fortnum and Mason would not have been nearly as grand. "Twenty pounds of tobacco! Twenty pounds of tea! A new gun! A new net! A carton of cigarettes for my Kabloona" — and, aside, in a not–too–*sotto voce* stage whisper — "His pipe stinks!" to convulse his audience.

From time to time, as the pile of goods on the floor rose, he'd ask: "How much?" meaning, how much money had he left? "Ah

His face streaked with sweat and blood, John Akana carries a heavy load of caribou meat to camp.

yes, thread for the wife. And needles. And a new pressure stove." Rosie trailed behind her master, meek and quiet. It was a perfect example of male dominance in Inuit society. But since I shared their tent, I happened to know that this was merely a front. For days prior to the trip, Rosie had carefully programmed Ekalun to buy precisely what she needed and wanted.

When he was down to five dollars, he said: "That I'll take in cash! One might need it," and all laughed. That would be his initial stake for the all-night poker game.

Ekalun was sleepy and sour when we returned home next day. "How did the game go?" I asked, not too tactfully. The five dollars were gone. And his lighter. And the recently repaired Swiss watch. "*Ayornamat.* (It can't be helped.)" He shrugged.

We lacked fat. The spring caribou were thin after their long migration and our main food, *mipku*, dried caribou meat, was leathery and lean. We ate pounds of it each day, yet were forever hungry. Living on an exclusive protein, fatless diet took its toll. We tired easily, and after a month developed the first signs of protein poisoning: diarrhea and swollen feet. As soon as we could supplement our lean-meat diet with fat fish, we felt fine again.

Camp life in summer was quiet and relaxed. Our nets gave us plenty of whitefish and the odd char. Short trips by canoe provided a few seals. In the past, the Bathurst Inlet people had hunted seals only in winter and spring; they used kayaks primarily to kill migrating caribou at river crossings. Ancient patterns persisted; summer simply was not their seal-hunting season and we lived very well on fish alone.

We moved outdoors. The women cooked on open fires, surrounded by a mass of dwarf willow and heather, serving as both fuel and windbreak, and when the food was ready we'd all sit together, eat, chat, and swat mosquitoes. Weeks merged into months; season followed season; my other life seemed remote, unreal. Ekalun had unobtrusively but expertly remodeled me. I now conformed, and early problems and frictions did not recur.

At first my curiosity and my questions had riled him, for in his culture questions were considered intrusive. Nor did they ask me questions, including the most obvious ones: Why had I come? What was I doing? How long would I stay? At first I assumed they simply didn't care. Later I found that they were intensely interested, but much too polite to ask. Then I talked about myself, my family, my life, and since I had broached it, they then could ask questions and asked them eagerly.

To some questions there were no intelligible answers. Ekalun asked me once about Montreal and how many people live there and I said: "Three million." How much is three million? Ekalun wanted to know. He had never seen more than perhaps a hundred people. More than all the caribou in the world, more than all the pebbles on our beach, I said. He thought that over for a while and then he smiled one of his sardonic smiles and said: "Too many!"

At an old campsite, I found a foot (30-cm)-long stick, the spindle of a fire drill. I showed it to Ekalun. He told me what it was, I pretended ignorance and, rather than waste time explaining, Ekalun made a simple version of the fire drill and showed me how it worked. This put him into a reminiscent mood; he told of travels long ago to a remote valley to pick up "fire stones," the iron pyrite that, struck together, produced sparks that caught on lightly oiled willow catkin fluff or arctic cotton tinder and were blown into a flame. It took about five minutes to produce fire by friction with a fire drill, Ekalun said, and only moments with the "fire stones."

From then on, rather than ask questions and annoy, I brought back from my long walks all artifacts I found — broken tools, worked bone, thimbles made of leather, a broken blubber pounder of musk-ox horn — and if I judged the moment and the mood propitious, I showed my finds to Rosie and Ekalun, like a child showing treasures to its parents.

It often worked. The small bone tube, brown with age and cracked, made of the leg bone of a goose was used, long ago, to suck fresh water off spring ice. That brought back memories of a trip on spring ice nearly half a century ago, when both were starving and their few dogs were near death. Ekalun had spotted a seal far out on the flooded ice and had crawled toward it through the icy water, imitating seal movements and behavior with such perfection that the seal thought he was a seal. It took more than an hour. His body went numb with cold; he dared not throw the harpoon. He crawled right up to the seal and killed it. Rosie, then about fifteen years old and just married, rushed up with the dogs. They ate the seal and lived.

Fall came, but no fat caribou for winter food, for clothing. We walked far inland. No caribou. We ascended the Hood River. No caribou. And suddenly Ekalun knew. The caribou, he said, are on the islands. We drove to the islands and the caribou were there. How had he known? Experience? Intuition? A good guess? I asked and got no answer. He simply knew. The men hunted. We took several boatloads of meat, fat, and skins back to camp. The rest we cached under heavy stones, to be picked up by dog team in winter.

The racks at camp were full of drying meat; slabs of back fat filled the caches. The char were returning to the rivers; our nets were heavy with fish. This was the vital harvest season of fall, to gather supplies until seal hunting began again in winter.

Snow fell on the mountains. Ice glazed the ponds. Winter was near. George would bring me by boat to Baychimo. An Arctic research vessel would stop there and take me "out."

The last night, Rosie rummaged in a bag and produced a pair of exquisite sealskin slippers, lined with the down-soft fur of an arctic hare. "These are for your wife," she said. "Tell her it is to thank her that she let you come to live with us." In the morning Ekalun saw me off. As I stepped into the boat, he gave me a small parcel. "This is for you, Kabloo, so you will remember us." George pushed off and I opened the parcel. In it was a 3-inch (7-cm)-high carving of an Inuk man in full fur regalia — Ekalun, the king of the chess set.

SLED DOGS AND DOG SLEDS

Inuit were great travelers. Ekalun of Bathurst Inlet was thoroughly familiar with a region bigger than Belgium. The explorer-scientist Graham W. Rowley lived at Igloolik, northern Hudson Bay, fifty years ago and found that there almost every Inuk knew "the country within a radius of 300 miles [480 km] or so. A comparable figure in an English village before the First World War would probably be about five miles [8 km] — one sixtieth the distance, or nearly one four-thousandth the area."

The Inuit traveled to hunt and to visit, and they traveled from a spirit of curiosity and adventure. Their legendary heroes, like Kivioot, were Ulysses-like travelers. A few years before I went to live with the Polar Inuit, two men in their fifties left the settlement with their dog teams in winter, sledged north to the very top of Greenland, enduring vicious storms and temperatures that at times fell to −58°F (−50°C), crossed over to Ellesmere Island, and returned many months later after a trip of about 2,500 miles (4000 km). Had a white "explorer" made such a trip, he would have been hailed as a hero, his achievement immortalized in books. The Inuit thought nothing of it. I heard about it by chance and asked one of the men why they had made this immense journey. He shrugged. "Just to see," he said.

When George Hakungak and Jessie got married, they took off on a three-month honeymoon walk with two pack dogs, a tent,

Camp children play with the husky pups and also look after them.

Every morning, weather permitting, the hunters from Ekalun's camp sledged to the ice to hunt seals. The trip took two hours each way.

On the sea ice of Maxwell Bay, the Inuit shot a large polar bear, skinned it, cut off the great haunches for us, and then turned the twenty-nine famished, slavering huskies loose. They ripped and gulped and fought, a ravening, blood-smeared pack of hounds from hell. Each dog ate 10 to 15 pounds (4.5 to 6.75 kg) of meat and fat. They gorged until their bellies sagged, and then rushed back for more. We camped, for after such a gargantuan feast the bloated dogs could only rest and digest, and for days after we traveled in a miasmic fog of dog farts.

In early summer, meltwater floods the sea ice, softening the paws of the dogs, and the water-eroded, needle-sharp ice cuts the dogs' tender feet. The Inuit then make bag-like sealskin booties for their dogs and tie them on fairly loosely so as not to cut off circulation. The dogs detest the booties. They look embarrassed and aggrieved and try to flick them off. When an eleven-dog team flicks off its forty-four booties, travel is extremely slow, so Inuit watch their dogs keenly and any dog that tries to shed its footwear gets a sharp crack with the 30-foot (9-m) whip.

In summer, the Inuit used the huskies as pack dogs. Each dog carried pack saddles, big sausage-shaped pouches, hanging down on either side, nearly to the ground. A dog could carry about 40 pounds (18 kg). When families migrated overland, the dogs carried the heavy items, such as the meat supply (and sometimes ate it), while the Inuit shouldered the bulkier loads, tents and sleeping skins. Huskies love to pull sleds; after fighting and mating, it is their main mission in life. But they do not like to carry loads. Their fur is thick and they overheat, and then head with great enthusiasm for any lake or river for a cooling bath, getting everything soaking wet.

The typical dog sled, the *qamutiiq* or *komatik*, now has two broad wooden runners, 2.5 inches (6 cm) thick, and is 12 inches (30 cm) high and from 12 to 30 feet (3.6 to 9.2 m) long. It is up-curved at the front and covered with closely spaced crossbars lashed

Sled dogs haul a killed polar bear to camp in 1967.

Jessie and Karetak watch as George skins a wolf. Its skin will be made into parka ruffs.

to the runners with sealskin thong or nylon line. The runners are shod with long strips of iron.

In former days, the Inuit sled was usually smaller. Wood, in most regions of the Arctic, was rare and precious. The runners were made of whale bone or of narwhal tusks, where available, or from pieces of driftwood, shod with strips of bone or caribou antler cut into flat sections and fastened to the wood with bone pegs or rivets of native copper. Inuit from as far away as northern Victoria Island traveled hundreds of miles to timber stands in sheltered river valleys of Canada's mainland tundra to obtain wood for sleds and kayaks. These trips often lasted half a year and more.

When the normal raw materials for sled building (wood, whale bone, ivory, baleen, or bone) were lacking, the ingenious Inuit could still construct a sled. They shaped runners out of soaked seal or musk-ox hides. Frozen solid, the runners kept their shape until the first thaw. Rock-hard frozen fish, long strips of frozen meat, or leg bones of caribou were used as transverse bars, all tied together with sealskin thong or plaited caribou sinew. This made a serviceable conveyance that, in addition, had a unique advantage: in times of dearth, the sled could be eaten.

The ideal runner shoeing was bone from the lower jaw of the bowhead whale: dense, hard, yet minutely pitted to hold the vital glaze. Before starting in the morning, the sled runners were iced.

Water was warmed, strips of snow were quickly dipped into it and the icy mush spread on the runners. It was planed smooth with a snow knife and coated by dipping a piece of polar-bear fur into lukewarm water and sliding it quickly over the runner, giving it an even, smooth glaze so that the great heavy sled slid smoothly over snow and ice.

In the central and western Arctic, whale bone was rare, and sled runners were covered with mud. Peaty earth was dug up in fall with a hoe made of a curved piece of caribou antler. In early winter, the black earth was boiled; kneaded into a thick, hot paste; and spread evenly on the runners, where it froze stone-hard. It lasted all winter, holding the glaze well, but when we traveled over rough ice the mud plaster sometimes cracked and crumbled. This happened when I made a long hunting trip with Peter Agliogoitok of Bathurst Inlet. His runner hit a rock and a hand-broad piece of mud shoeing broke out. Peter had no earth along. Instead, he boiled a big pot of thick oatmeal porridge, which was used to replace the missing mud on the runner; we ate the rest.

The husky's heyday was probably in the 1920s and 1930s. The introduction of firearms made it easier for Inuit to procure ample food from the then still fairly abundant game resources. The long traplines Inuit ran to pay for southern goods they now considered essential, such as guns, ammunition, kettles, flour, tea, and sugar, made it important to have large dog teams. Big teams became status symbols. In the Canadian Arctic alone, more than 20,000 huskies were busy pulling sleds.

Just as the motor-driven canoe edged the kayak into oblivion in most of the Arctic, so did the fast snowmobile replace the husky in the North. By 1970, only 2,000 huskies were left in the Canadian Arctic. Now, as working dogs of the Inuit, they are nearly extinct, except in Greenland. The Polar Inuit remain faithful to many traditions, including the use of sled dogs. A local law forbids the use of snowmobiles; all hunters still travel by dog team.

I'm glad. Sled dogs were part of the living magic of the North in a way that snowmobiles will never be. I have traveled thousands of miles by dog team and we were as one with the earth and the sky: the endless space, the running dogs; we were free in a world without time.

I had walked far inland and it was late at night when I returned to Ekalun's camp. The dry snow creaked and groaned with every step, but when I stopped, there was an awesome silence. A brilliant sliver of new moon hung in a sky of velvet black. Auroras danced and flared, great curtains of greenish light rising into heaven. Our tents glowed in the distance, deep yellow specks in the bluish void. And suddenly the huskies howled and keened, their wolf-like heads raised to the soaring spectral fires in the sky, and they filled the Arctic night with a chorus of wildness and melancholy and longing.

SEALS: THE STAFF OF ARCTIC LIFE

Here I stand,
Humble, with outstretched arms.
For the spirit of the air
Lets glorious food sink down to me.
Here I stand
Surrounded with great joy.
And this time it was an old dog seal
Starting to blow through his breathing hole.
I, little man,
Stood upright above it,
And with excitement became
Quite long of body,
Until I drove my harpoon in the beast
And tethered it to
My harpoon line!

— Hymn to the air spirit by Igpakuhak of Victoria Island,
recorded in 1924 by Knud Rasmussen

I tried it once — and only once. I had read so much about it, had watched it, had even written about the astounding patience and concentration of Inuit hunting seals at agloos, their breathing holes. In January 1916, the anthropologist Diamond Jenness wrote about Victoria Island Inuit: "The calm weather had drawn every hunter out to the ice-field... They were standing like pillars over their individual seal holes, scarcely daring to raise their heads lest they should alarm the seals beneath."

Sometimes they stood like that for days and nights. Ugarang, a Baffin Island Inuk, returned to the camp where the explorer Charles Francis Hall lived in 1862, "having been out two days and one night over a seal hole." And he missed the seal! All he said was: "I go tomorrow morning again." It was January and the temperature was –30°F (–49°C).

In winter and in spring at Bathurst Inlet, Ekalun and his sons went seal hunting every day weather permitted. It was a two-hour trip by dog team to the sealing grounds. Then the men and their trained huskies searched for suitable agloos. Each man stood statue-still above a seal's breathing hole, and the long wait in bitterly cold weather began.

By frequent observation, I had the theory down pat. Now, I felt, I should find out what it was like in practice. I found an agloo (far away from the Inuit), inserted an idlak, attached a colored tassel to its top, bent slightly (I cannot stand, in Inuit fashion, like a three-quarter-closed jackknife), stared at the tassel, and waited.

After fifteen minutes, my attention shifted, my mind wandered.

I itched in several places. After standing totally still for an hour, I felt cramped and miserable. The wind picked up and, at –4°F (–20°C — not a particularly cold day), I began to feel nagging chills here and there. I thought of home. I recited poems. From time to time, with an effort, I forced myself to concentrate on that tassel, to think of nothing or, at least, to think only of the coming of the seal.

After two hours, I had run out of poetry and patience. After three hours, I felt stiff, cold, and exhausted. The total lack of movement, the absence of any stimuli, grated on my nerves. After six hours, I gave up. I was cold, creaky, cranky, and intensely annoyed with myself, but that was about as much as I could take. Yet the Inuit did this nearly every day for ten to fifteen hours, and sometimes they got a seal and often they did not. Their concentration was total, their patience endless, for to Inuit (and polar bears) the seal was everything. I once asked Inuterssuaq of the Polar Inuit, "What is the most important thing in life?" He reflected for a while, then smiled and said: "Seals, for without them we could not live."

George Best, captain and chronicler of Martin Frobisher's 1578 expedition to Baffin Island, said of the Inuit: "These people...

With endless patience, Apalinguaq, a Polar Inuk, waits for a seal to surface in its breathing hole in the ice.

hunte for their dinners… even as the Beare." Inuit and polar bear do, in fact, use similar seal-hunting methods. Both wait with infinite patience at agloos, hoping for seals to surface.

In late spring and early summer, seals bask upon the ice, and Inuit and polar bears synchronize their patient stalk with the sleep-wake rhythm of the seals. Typically, a seal sleeps for a minute or so, wakes, looks carefully all around to make certain no enemy is near, and then, satisfied that all is safe, falls asleep for another minute or two. The moment the seal slumps in sleep, the bear advances. The instant the seal looks up, the bear freezes into immobility, camouflaged by its yellowish-white fur. At 20 yards (18 m) the bear pounces, a deadly blur across the ice, and grabs and kills the seal.

In the eastern Arctic, Inuit stalk a seal on the ice hidden behind a portable hunting screen, now of white cloth, formerly of bleached seal or caribou skin. In the central Arctic, Inuit do not use the screen. Instead they employ a method known to Inuit from Siberia to Greenland: they approach the seal by pretending to be a seal. They slither across the snow while the seal sleeps. When it wakes, the hunter stops and makes seal-like movements. To successfully impersonate a seal, a hunter told me, "you have to think like a seal." It is a hunt that requires great skill and endurance.

They hunted seals at their agloos, they stalked them with screens on the ice. They waited for them at the floe edge and they harpooned them from kayaks. They hunted seals in fall on ice so thin it bent beneath the hunter's weight. They hunted them in the bluish darkness of the winter night, and they invented and perfected an entire arsenal of ingenious weapons and devices to hunt the seal. For, to Inuit, the seal was life, and their greatest goddess was Sedna, mother of seals and whales.

A few inland groups lived nearly exclusively on caribou. The Mackenzie Delta Inuit are beluga hunters. Many Inuit of the Bering Sea and Bering Strait region live primarily on walrus. In Greenland and Labrador, Inuit hunted harp seals and hooded seals (the Polar Inuit drum Masautsiaq made for me as a farewell present is covered with the throat membrane of a hooded seal). But, for most Inuit, two seal species were of truly vital importance: the large bearded seal that weighs up to 600 pounds (270 kg), and the smaller — up to 180 pounds (81 kg) — but numerous ringed seal. These two seals were the basis of human life in the Arctic.

I spent the spring of 1975 with the walrus hunters of Little Diomede Island in Bering Strait, between Alaska and Siberia. Among our crew was Tom, Jr., or Junior as everyone called him, the eleven-year-old son of Tom Menadelook, captain of the large walrus-skin-covered umiak, the traditional hunting boat of the Diomeders. On one of our trips into the pack ice, Junior shot his first seal. His father was typically gruff and curt, but we could see that he was pleased and proud. The crew made much of the boy and he glowed in their praise. That night, his mother, Mary Menadelook, cut the seal into many pieces, and following ancient custom, the boy took meat to all the households in the village, including to my shack, thus symbolically feeding us all. He was a man now, a provider, who shared in traditional Inuit fashion.

Seal meat and fat, raw or cooked, was the main food of most Inuit and their sled dogs. The high-calorie blubber gave strength, warmth, and endurance to the people; it heated them from within. Rendered into seal oil, it burned in their semicircular soapstone lamps, cooked their meals, heated their homes, and, most importantly, melted fresh-water ice or snow into drinking water. Lack of blubber meant hunger, icy, dark homes, and excruciating thirst.

Although Inuit were hardy and inured to cold, and dressed in superb fur clothing, their high-calorie, high-protein meat-fat diet also helped them to withstand the rigors of winter, for it raised their basal metabolic rate by 20 to 40 percent. Fortunately for the Inuit, blubber is a beneficial fat. Scientists were fascinated that Inuit who, a recent study says, "traditionally obtained about 40 percent of their calories from fat," had, in the past, no heart disease because their diet "although high in fat, is low in saturated fat… and that presumably explains their freedom from disease."

Seal oil, in the past, was stored in sealskin pokes and kept in stone caches, safe from arctic foxes, for spring and summer use. At Bathurst Inlet, Ekalun once showed me a great, solitary stone pillar, too sheer and high for bears or foxes to climb, upon which, in the past, Inuit had stored pokes of oil (they used a sled as a ladder to climb to the top). Even now, after decades of disuse, the distinctive, cloying smell of ancient seal oil clung to the pillar.

The Inuit of Little Diomede eat seal oil with nearly all their meals. When they have to go to hospital in Nome or Anchorage, they take a bottle of seal oil along, because without it, they say, "food just doesn't taste right." Seal oil is their main preservative: they store in it the thousands of murre eggs they collect in summer, and bags of greens — and both keep reasonably fresh for about a year. They even had a type of chewing gum made of solidified seal oil and willow catkins, and a mixture of whipped blubber and cloudberries is known in Alaska as "Eskimo ice cream."

Inuit used sealskins to make their tents and cover their kayaks, and women made from them durable summer clothing. Sealskin boots, the shaft of ringed-seal leather, the sole of extremely durable bearded-seal leather, are light, comfortable, and lasting. Tataga, Akpaleeapik's wife, made a beautiful pair for me and I wore them for fifteen winters. The *avatak*, the float at the end of the harpoon line, is made of sealskin, and so are the bags in which oil, food, and clothing are stored.

The very long gut of the bearded seal was carefully cleaned and scraped. From it Inuit made waterproof clothing, sails for their umiaks, and the parchment-like windows of their winter homes. Inuterssuaq and Naduq returned from a summer trip to Littleton Island with about 2,000 eider eggs, poured hundreds of them into cleaned seal guts, draped them like pink sausages over poles, air-dried them, and later we ate slices of these taffy-colored egg sausages like candy with our tea.

Thimbles were made from thick bearded-seal leather, and thong for dog-team harnesses and traces. Seal thong was the Inuk's harpoon line and the guy rope that held his tent; it was the tumpline with which he carried loads in sealskin bags, and with it he lashed the load onto his dog sled. And from long thong lines in northern Greenland, strung up the mountainside from stone cairn to stone cairn, dangled dozens of baleen snares to capture passing hares.

Seal bones were carved into children's toys or into *ajagait,* skill-testing ring-and-pin games, and with the phalangeal bones of seals Inuit played *inugaq,* a game akin to dice.

All animals, Inuit once believed, had souls and feelings, just like humans — were, in fact, our distant kin. They allowed themselves to be killed; it was a kindness they rendered to people who treated them with respect. To lead a safe and successful life, the Netsilik Inuk Qaqortingneq told Rasmussen: "I must never offend Nuliajuk or Narssuk [the goddess of the sea — also called Sedna — and the god of the air]. I must never offend the souls of animals."

At night when we returned from the sealing grounds and knelt in the tent around the great platter of steaming seal meat, Ekalun murmured an ancient prayer. He spoke to the soul of the seal and thanked it for giving us food and for a moment, in that steam-filled tent, men, women, and children dressed in furs in the yellow light of the seal-oil lamp, we were in a primal, deeply mystical communion with the spirits of animals and nature.

The seal-oil lamp gave the Inuit warmth, cooked their meals, and dried their clothing.

The great sea
Has set me adrift,
It moves me as a weed in a great river,
Earth and the great weather
Move me,
Have carried me away
And move my inward parts with joy.

— Poem of ecstasy by Uvanuk, a famous woman shaman among the Igloolik Inuit in the 1920s, recorded by Knud Rasmussen

CHAPTER SIX

THE BELUGA HUNTERS

IN PREHISTORIC TIMES — A MERE 200 YEARS AGO — THE MACKENZIE
River delta and adjacent coasts were the richest, most populous
region in what is now the Canadian Arctic. About 30,000 bowhead
whales summered in the shallow Beaufort Sea, 50-ton (45-tonne)
feasts for hunters skillful and daring enough to kill them. There
were Dall's sheep in the mountains, moose in the valleys, musk-
oxen on the tundra, and in summer vast herds of caribou on the
wind-swept coastal plains.

Seals were common. Great polar bears patrolled the ice, and fat
Barren Ground grizzlies patrolled the land. Here were the breeding
grounds of much of North America's waterfowl: the myriad tundra
lakes were speckled with ducks and geese, loons and swans. Rivers
and lakes were rich in fish: char and inconnu, and immense shoals
of herring and fat whitefish.

Most important to the Inuit of this region were the milky-white
beluga whales that arrived each year in large pods in late June at the
edge of the Mackenzie estuary and remained for six to seven weeks
in its shallow, sun-warmed bays and inlets, where they were
relatively easy to hunt. The people were the Mackenzie Inuit, the
"Beluga Hunters," as archaeologist Robert McGhee of the Canadian
Museum of Civilization has called them. When he dug trenches
through the thick refuse layers at Kittigazuit, the main village of the
Mackenzie Inuit, "87 percent [of all bones] were of beluga." These
Inuit took all that a bounteous nature offered, but the beluga —
large, easily killed, and abundant — was their favorite prey.

While in other parts of the Canadian North the average
population density was one person to every 250 square miles (648
km²), 2,500 to 4,000 Mackenzie Inuit lived in settlements near the
river mouth. Inuit camps, specks of humanity scattered across the
vastness of the Arctic, were usually home to a few families, perhaps
50 people. Kittigazuit, the main village of the Beluga Hunters, had
a summer population of 800 to 1,000 people.

Among the Inuit at Kittigazuit at the turn of this century was an
orphan boy named Nuligak who lived with his crippled
grandmother. "Because I was an orphan and a poor one at that, my
mind was always alert to the happenings around me. Once my eyes
had seen something, it was never forgotten." He became a famous
hunter and, in old age, wrote *I, Nuligak*, the story of his life,
wonderfully vivid glimpses of a long-vanished world.

*The 1985 summer camp of
the Beluga Hunters at the
head of the Mackenzie
River delta.*

"The Inuit of those days [about 1900, when Nuligak was five years old] lived on game and fish only, and fished and hunted on a grand scale." The 900-yard (823-m)-long Kittigazuit beach "was hardly large enough for all the kayaks drawn up there," and the moment belugas were spotted "a swarm of kayaks was launched. At the great whale hunts I remember there was such a large number of kayaks that when the first had long disappeared from view, more and more were just setting out… Clever hunters killed five, seven belugas, and after the hunt the shore was covered with whale carcasses… Once I heard elders say that three hundred whales had been taken."

The great driftwood racks and stages were packed with drying meat, sealskin pokes were filled with fat, ample food for "*kaivitivik*, the time of dancing and rejoicing which began with the departure of the sun and ended with its return," Nuligak recalled. "In those days the Inuit could make marvelous things": puppets and toy animals, activated by baleen strings and springs, that hopped and danced across the floor of their great winter meeting hall, while Nuligak and the other children watched in wonder. "There was such an abundance of meals, games, and things to admire that these sunless weeks sped by as if they had been only a few days."

Until 1888, the Mackenzie Inuit had little contact with the outside world. That year the southern whalers came and the ancient, unchanging world of the Beluga Hunters collapsed in agony, despair, disease, and death. "Aboriginal Mackenzie Eskimo culture could probably be considered to have become extinct between 1900 and 1910," Robert McGhee noted with scientific detachment.

In 1888, whalers reached the Beaufort Sea, last sanctuary of the rapidly declining bowhead whales. Six years later, 2,000 people wintered at Herschel Island, west of the Delta, soon known as the "Sodom of the North." It was the largest "town" in northwestern Canada, inhabited, according to a Nome, Alaska, newspaper report, "by demons of debauchery and cruelty," the scene, according to horrified missionaries, of "bacchanalian orgies."

Nuligak's memories are less lurid. He remembered the whalers more as friends than as fiends. "White men and Inuit played games together, as well as hunting side by side. We played baseball and wrestled. We danced in the Eskimo fashion to the sound of many drums."

Unintentionally, though, the whalers brought death to the long-isolated Inuit. They needed great amounts of fresh meat. Musk-oxen vanished from the land. Few bowhead whales remained. In 1914, the Royal North-West Mounted Police reported that caribou were virtually extinct in the Mackenzie region. By then, the Beluga Hunters, too, were nearing extinction.

As the plague had ravaged medieval Europe, measles and smallpox epidemics wiped out the Beluga Hunters, who lacked immunity to southern diseases. Of 3,000 people, fewer than 100 survived. In 1900, nearly 1,000 Inuit camped at Kittigazuit. In 1906, a single family remained in this village of death and decay.

Into the vacuum created by the demise of the Mackenzie people flowed Inuit from as far west as Alaska's Seward Peninsula, and even Yuit and Chukchi from Siberia. Traders and trappers came from the south. And whalers from all over the world and from every social stratum — the dregs of San Francisco's slums and a Count Bülow, a remote cousin of the chancellor of the German Reich; Spanish-speaking Africans; Chinese coolies; and people from the Polynesian Islands — settled in the region and "went native." One day in the town of Inuvik an Inuk girl, a sociology student, asked me: "Where are you from originally?" I told her I was Baltic German, born in Riga, Latvia. "Well, for heaven's sake!" she exclaimed. "My grandfather came from Riga."

These people, then, part Inuit, part everyone, became the new Beluga Hunters, following, to some extent, the millennial customs and traditions of the nearly extinct Mackenzie Inuit. The changes wrought through the coming of the whalers were enormous, but some things had not changed: the coming of the belugas, the need for food, the ancient rhythm of camp life through the seasons.

Even the remnants of this ancient whaling culture seemed fated to fade away. Professor Vagn Flyger of the University of Maryland, who studied the Beluga Hunters in 1961 and 1962, predicted confidently that "Eskimo whale camps will soon be no more," and Nuligak wrote in the 1950s that "the Inuit eat white man's food nowadays." In the late 1970s, the oil companies came, their made-in-Japan module headquarters, with gleaming offices and dining rooms, with swimming pools and cinemas, squatting on the tundra, with their spacecraft-like drilling rigs far out in the Beaufort Sea, all backed by multibillion-dollar exploration budgets. Yet, "the old way of life" persisted. When I went to join the Beluga Hunters in the summer of 1985, twenty-five families from the towns of Tuktoyaktuk, Inuvik, and Aklavik had "returned to the land," to ancient camps along the coast where Inuit had lived and hunted belugas for thousands of years. "From time immemorial this has been our life," said Nuligak.

Once I came to Inuit camps by dog team or, in summer, by boat. Now I came by helicopter. As we approached East Whitefish Station, a traditional camp not far from the now abandoned Kittigazuit, I saw two tents, one new and gleaming white, the other weather-stained, upon a bluff above a broad sand-and-pebble beach. Beyond, white specks zigzagged across the silt-brown waters of Kugmallit Bay, boats of the last Beluga Hunters in pursuit of whales.

The pilot landed far from camp so as not to blow down the tents, and helped to unload my gear. Then the machine rose with a shrill metallic whine and swooped away across the tundra. Suddenly it

A pod of beluga whales.

was quiet. The wind soughed gently through the waist-high willows
and from the beach came the rhythmic growling of wave-rolled
pebbles. I walked slowly toward the tents, as always beset by worry
about the welcome I would receive. A woman came out of the white
tent, her round face smiling and friendly. "I'm Lena," she said.
"Come and have tea." It was the traditional greeting of a hospitable
people. "I'm Fred Bruemmer," I introduced myself. "I know," she
said. "I've seen your books." Vain, like most authors, I hoped she
would say more, but the books were never again mentioned.

Lena's large tent, taut canvas over a wooden frame, was spotless,
and all entered in stocking feet, leaving their sandy-muddy rubber
boots or running shoes on planks outside. Its furnishings were
modern, but its interior layout was nearly identical with that of
Inuit dwellings of 2,000 years ago. The back of the tent, where
formerly the sleeping platform would have been, was occupied by
sheet-covered mattresses. Bedrolls and sleeping bags lay against the
wall. Plank shelves held dishes, pots, pans, and a large assortment
of spices and condiments. Where once the soapstone seal-oil lamp
would have stood, there was now an efficient sheet-metal stove
burning split driftwood. The tea was delicious. "Of course," Lena
said. "It's made with clean water. No chlorine!"

While Lena talked, she kneaded dough and then baked bannock
in a heavy cast-iron pan upon the stove with the unhurried
efficiency of a person used to having surprise visitors and many
people at most meals. Later, at the peak of the whaling season, she
often fed sixteen to twenty people twice a day. Two of her six
children were in camp — Erika, fourteen, now playing with her
cousin Sharon on the beach, and Dennis, thirteen, hunting with
his father on Kugmallit Bay.

The tent flap opened, and Mary Aviugana, Lena's sister-in-law,
called Lulu by nearly everyone in camp, came in, trailed by two of

her children, Maggie, three, and Mandy, two. The latter was called "Bombay" because, Lulu explained, "when she was real little she looked just like a kid from Bombay I saw in a magazine." Both children ate lots of warm bannock with butter and jam, and then, full and jam-coated, tried to sidle out of the tent. Lulu, a relaxed but firm mother, caught both and wiped the hands and faces of the two squirming children despite their moues and protests. "Now go and play outside," she said, and the little adventurers vanished.

Lena baked and cooked and talked, but part of her mind was with her man and the whales in the bay. She often left the tent and scanned Kugmallit Bay with powerful binoculars. Usually quiet and placid, she suddenly burst into the tent, flushed with excitement: "Alex's got a whale!" she cried. "Alex's got a whale!"

The first beluga of the season had been taken from our camp. Far out upon the bay a boat towing a whale was heading for our beach. We stood upon the flensing beach, which was permeated with the oil and blood of hecatombs of whales, and where for centuries Inuit women and children had awaited the return of the hunters. The cloying sweetish-rancid smell of ancient blubber hung over the beach, and the pebbles beneath the massive driftwood stages were amber-brown with ancient oil.

Alex Aviugana and his brother Rudolph, Lulu's husband, tied a long rope around the whale's peduncle and all heaved in rhythm to haul the 2,500-pound (1125-kg) carcass closer to shore. The body either did not budge or, buoyed by a wave, slipped suddenly and we all went sprawling, the women and children screaming with laughter. Finally, when the whale was really stuck, Alex and Rudolph spiraled a rope around its body, and, using this ancient but efficient method, older perhaps than Archimedes, we rolled the inert carcass close to the beach.

Lena and Lulu, using razor-sharp ulus (the blades now made of steel and formerly of sharpened slate), cut 50-pound (22.5-kg) slabs of muktuk, skin plus blubber, from the whale. They made handhold slits into the oil-slippery pieces, and the men carried them ashore and placed them on the driftwood stages. The women then carved with speed and amazing precision the black, coarse-grained meat from the bones, and in less than two hours the gleaming white whale had vanished. Its skeleton lay in a crimson cove, as blood-frothy wavelets rolled onto the beach. In the distance, convoys of tug-towed barges carried multimillion-dollar cargoes to the drilling rigs in the Beaufort Sea.

The men sank the whale skeleton far from shore, food for crabs and shrimps, then cleaned the boat and washed their knives and greasy, bloody hands and hip waders with liquid Palmolive soap.

Supper was ready when we came to camp. Lena, as usual, had invited everyone. She spread a large, clean tablecloth upon the carpeted tent floor. The Inuit kneeled or sat cross-legged around it

Lena Aviugana covers whale meat with onion rings. A little niece is kept away from the hot stove in a homemade Jolly Jumper.

in comfortable ease. With my long legs and stiff knees, I reclined awkwardly, like a rheumatic Roman. Even after forty years of living in Lapp and Inuit tents, I'm still not comfortable on the floor.

Before the meal, Alex said a prayer. While we sat with bowed heads, he thanked the Lord for the food and for the whale he had killed, which was now part of our supper. The Beluga Hunters who had camped here long ago also offered up prayers of gratitude after successful hunts. They thanked the spirit of the whale for allowing itself to be killed and providing the people with food.

Like all of Lena's meals, this one was varied and abundant, a mixture of land and city food. She baked nearly every day and we had fresh bread, buns, bannock, and doughnuts. The main course was whale meat, dark, stringy and lean, broiled with masses of onion rings and seasoned with salt, pepper, and a liberal dash of Worcestershire sauce. We had a huge platter heaped with muktuk, eaten by most with HP sauce or ketchup, and bundles of smoked herring, inconnu, and whitefish, leathery but delicious, fresh from the smokehouses on the beach. In addition, there were baked beans, boiled potatoes, rice, and canned tomatoes, and a large dish of lasagna made by Lulu. We drank lots of tea with the meal, and for dessert we had buns with butter and jam, Jell-O, more tea, and tinned cookies from Denmark.

The meal was leisurely and relaxed. Alex talked little about the hunt. But Dennis, still aquiver with excitement and immensely proud to have hunted with his father, told Erika and me in vivid detail the story of the chase: the zigs and zags of the pursuing boat, the noise of bullets whining off the water, the harpooning of the whale, and finally the kill. The language was English. Inuktitut is dying out in the western Arctic. Old people still speak it. Alex and Lena understood it but rarely spoke it. And young adults and children knew only a few words and phrases picked up from grandparents or learned in school.

Alex was in a mellow mood. A powerfully built, darkly handsome man, he was usually quiet, nearly taciturn. Now, buoyed by the successful hunt, he reminisced about the hunts of long ago, about his youth "in the Delta." Nearly all Inuit then lived in camps. In late June, they came to the ancient coastal camps to hunt whales and net fish, vital winter provisions for themselves and their sled dogs. In September, the people scattered across the vastness of the Delta and to "bush camps" to the east and west. "We trapped all winter," Alex recalled, "and then, in spring, we went by dog team to Aklavik to sell our furs. We bought grub and ammunition and went again to the whaling camps. Some years that beach below was covered with tents and we took twenty or thirty whales in a day."

Now Alex was an Inuvik building contractor and town councillor, and Rudolph had an electrical contracting business. For ten months of the year the brothers were busy city entrepreneurs, immersed in estimates, supplies, and work. Each June they left their businesses and their comfortable city homes and returned to the ancient whaling camps at the edge of Kugmallit Bay. Why, I asked, did he make this costly trip at a time when he could be earning money in town? Alex shrugged. "I guess this is where I belong," he said. "Our people have always lived here in summer and hunted the beluga whales." Lena added another reason. "Camp life is good for the kids," she said. "It keeps them busy. There are too many problems in town, especially in summer when the schools are closed."

The camp absorbed me. I chopped wood. Dennis and I fetched water from Bum Lake near buttock-shaped Bum Hill. On rainy days, the children and I sat in Lena's spacious tent and played Snakes and Ladders, checkers, and many card games. The children played with the lightning speed of routine and the impatience of youth and were politely exasperated by my slowness and obtuseness. "Don't think so much, Fred," Erika urged. "Just play!" Lena played solitaire, while Alex repaired tools or motors, read the Bible, glancing at Lena's game from time to time and giving occasional quiet advice.

Time in camp had little meaning. All did what had to be done or what they felt like doing. I supplied Lena with firewood and went for long walks along this coast so rich in history, discovering remnants of ancient houses, once homes of the Beluga Hunters, graves, broken tools and weapons, and log-lined cold-storage cellars dug deep into the permafrost that still smelled of ancient blubber.

The children did their chores and played. Their favorite toy was an enormous crescent of Styrofoam washed ashore from one of the passing barges. It made a marvelously tippy teeter-totter, spilling kids, screaming with laughter, onto the sand. In the evening and during the luminous night, they played baseball on the beach or hide-and-go-seek near camp among the willow bushes. As I lay reading in my tent, I heard the rush of racing feet, a sharp twang as someone tripped over a guy rope of the tent, a hurried "Sorry, Fred!" as the feet raced on, and then a shout of triumph. (It took me back to my childhood in rural Latvia when we played the same game in the "white nights" of the North.) When all but one were caught or free, the children chanted: "Monkey, monkey in the tree / You come down / For you are free," an odd little rhyme for a treeless (and monkeyless) land.

Inuit from other whaling camps came for visits. One was Richard Binder from Inuvik, born on Richards Island "in the Delta." His grandmothers were Inuit. His maternal grandfather was a Lapp herder from Norway's Kautokeino region, who had driven reindeer from Alaska to the Delta. His paternal grandfather was the German trader at the Tree River post who was murdered by a young Inuk in the 1920s, a famous, starkly northern tragedy of

blood feuds and clashing cultures. The young Inuk was taken to
Herschel Island, tried, convicted, and hanged. "My grandfather
may have helped to hang him," Alex quietly remarked. "He was the
RCMP special constable at Herschel at the time."

Billy Day was the doyen of our camp, the head and soul of East
Whitefish Station. He arrived shortly after I did in a much-patched
22-foot (6-m) freighter canoe loaded to the gunwales with supplies
and people. With him came Maggie, his wife, and three of their
twelve children: Marsha, a joyous girl who played with Dennis,
Maggy, and Mandy; and two sons, Linley Day, called Baby Boy,
and Forest Day, called "Aba" (Father), who were as alike as twins
but could easily be told apart by one idiosyncrasy — Linley always
wore a hat, even in bed, I was told, and Forest never wore one, even
in pouring rain.

Billy Day, a stocky, broad-shouldered man, slow now and
deliberate but still powerful, his hair just beginning to gray, was an
old-timer, a "man of the Delta" where he had spent most of his life
hunting, fishing, and trapping. He was also president of Inuvialuit
Nunangat, the powerful Committee for Original Peoples'
Entitlement (COPE), which worked out the infinitely complex land-
claims settlements in the western Arctic with the government of
Canada. For much of the year Billy Day traveled between his office
in Inuvik and offices in Yellowknife and Ottawa, conferring with
lawyers and politicians and analyzing position papers. But in June,
when the belugas came, he returned to East Whitefish Station, put
up a much-used and much-mended tent upon the spot where he
had camped for nearly half a century, and resumed the life he loved.

He no longer hunted or fished. The boys did that and he had
taught them well. He and Maggie split, dried, and smoked the fish,
and "made muktuk." They cleaned the vitamin-rich, high-energy
whaleskin, boiled it in a cut-down 45-gallon (170-l) drum, and
preserved it in whale oil in large plastic pails, modern substitutes
for the sealskin pokes Billy Day used when he was young. They
worked slowly, unhurriedly, efficiently. Between work, they often
sat on a big log on the beach, smoked and talked quietly together,
or watched the great oil company ships that passed in the distance.

Billy Day's major project for the season was a new smokehouse.
It was built, a bit haphazardly, it seemed — a massive upright log
here, another there, buried deep into the sand, the interstices filled
with smaller logs. Nearly all the material came from the beach: the
logs for the palisade-like walls, the pieces of plywood and planking,
spikes and nails from an old pier washed ashore not far from camp.
Bent nails were carefully straightened and reused. In seven days the
smokehouse was finished, a massive structure built to last
generations.

I was happy at camp; I liked its timeless rhythm. The people
were very kind. Lena tried to fatten me, the children included me

*A giant drilling rig in the
Beaufort Sea is twenty
stories high.*

Forest Day harpoons a white whale while his brother Linley steers the boat.

in their games, Billy Day told me fascinating tales about old times in the Delta. Yet something was not quite right. There seemed to be a vague undercurrent of tension, of rejection. Alex, especially, seemed at times reserved to the point of coldness, and I wondered uneasily whether, unwittingly, I had broken a camp taboo.

Finally I screwed up my courage and asked Billy Day. He laughed, amused at so much naïveté. "Of course we're in a way unhappy that you are in camp," he said. "Whaling is a very sensitive issue. There are many powerful conservation groups who want to stop all whaling. So we worry how your pictures will be used."

A month earlier the oil companies had been unhappy about my presence for a similar reason. In 1984 and 1985, the National Film Board of Canada made six films about the Arctic from my slides. As the producer, Julie Stanfel, and I assembled the transparencies, there was one glaring lacuna: I had no pictures of industry in the North. The necessary permissions were obtained, and I spent weeks on the drilling vessels and artificial islands in the Beaufort Sea in a strange and (to me) alien world.

One drilling vessel, built for $250 million in Japan, was a futuristic town, twenty stories high, with luxurious accommodations for 108 people ("my" room had deep-pile carpets and a beautiful Hakata doll in a polished glass and mahogany case), a superb German chef, and a chief steward with a history degree from McGill University, who was a fervent admirer of Richard III and who scoffed at Shakespeare as a mere "Tudor hack." The vessel had two giant (nearly everything in this operation was both "giant" and horrendously expensive) distillation plants, each producing 40 tons (36 tonnes) of fresh water a day. Positioning of the vessel, drilling, analysis of data, shift change, crew rotation, and the myriad other operational details of this spacecraft-like vessel were recorded and regulated by the most modern computers on earth. To me it seemed as if I had entered the twenty-first century.

On all drilling platforms I was given every help and cooperation. I could go where I wanted, photograph what I wanted. For aerial pictures I got helicopters, for distant pictures I went aboard one of the giant (of course!) icebreakers: "Just let me know where you want to be," said the captain. (I felt somewhat inhibited by the knowledge that it cost $8,330 an hour to run the ship.) Yet beneath the kindness, the help, the generosity, I sensed a certain malaise and, late one night in the privacy of his cabin, a geologist told me the reason: "Of course we're worried about you being here. Just imagine something happens while you're here. Oil drilling in the Arctic is a very sensitive issue. We worry how your pictures will be used."

Whatever their apprehensions, the oil people and the Inuit were always friendly and I enjoyed my time on the futuristic drilling vessel and at the age-old whaling camp. The season was drawing to a close. Billy Day had to return to his office; Alex had to attend a conference in Calgary. I had as yet not gone whaling; the weather had been stormy, and Alex's closed cutter would have made it impossible to photograph the hunt. I also feared that, if I asked, he would turn me down. So I asked Billy Day if I could go out with his sons. "I'll think about it," he said, and I was fairly certain this meant

The bullroarer made by this Baffin Island Inuk makes a loud humming noise when whirled on a sinew line.

no. But an hour later Linley and Forest stopped at my tent. "You want to come whaling?" Linley asked. "Dad says it's okay." I rushed up to Day's tent to thank him. "It's against my better judgment," he grumbled. "Now go before I change my mind."

Linley steered the freighter canoe driven by a 35-horsepower motor. Forest checked the whaling gear. An avatak, a float, formerly an inflated sealskin and now a bright red plastic buoy, was attached by a rope to the harpoon shaft. The harpoon, now made of iron, was in former days carved from whalebone or antler. When he was certain the line was smoothly coiled, Forest stood beside his brother, rifle at the ready, keen and alert. A whale surfaced. He aimed, then lowered the gun. It was a female with a calf. The next few whales were also spared. They were small and probably females, and both boys knew their father would be angry if they killed a female whale.

A large whale surfaced near us, brilliant white in the brownish sea, and exhaled with a resounding "swoosh." Forest shot, but missed. The whale dived instantly and fled, but in this shallow bay, only a fathom deep, he left a telltale ripple track upon the water. He surfaced and Forest's next shot wounded the whale. The boat was close when the whale came up again. Forest threw the heavy harpoon, the barb struck, and the whale was doomed. The bobbing scarlet buoy now revealed its exact position. The next time the whale surfaced, Forest shot at close range, the whale thrashed briefly in his final flurry, the great heart-shaped fluke slammed the sea, and then he was still and dead. The chase had lasted twenty minutes. Linley and Forest reeved a rope around the beluga's fluke and towed it slowly toward shore, where the women and children waited, as untold generations before them had, for their men to return with the whale.

GAMES INUIT PLAY

Many toys and games are ancient and universal. In some of the oldest graves of Egypt, archaeologists have found little piles of peculiarly shaped bones. They are astragali, the tarsal bones of sheep and goats. Some 7,000 years old, these bones were the precursors of dice. They were used for gambling and, since fate and fortune are closely linked, the Greeks and Romans later used them also for astragalomancy, the divination of fate through the toss of bones.

In 1968, toward the end of my six-month trip around Labrador and arctic Quebec, I stayed in the village of Povungnituk on the northeast coast of Hudson Bay. I often visited Alacee Qingalik, the widow of Nanook, the man made famous by Robert Flaherty's 1921 film *Nanook of the North*. One day Alacee asked me whether I would like to see a game she used to play long ago. She produced a sizable bag of bones, the phalangeal bones of ringed seals. "I've had these since I was a little girl," she said.

Alacee Qingalik (right) and her friends play an ancient Inuit game with the phalangeal bones of ringed seals.

One evening Alacee and several elderly Inuit who still knew the game, called *inugaq*, got together and played it. Each player received a certain number of bones. With these he "built" the outlines of an igloo, complete with sleeping platform, men (long bones), women (short bones), and, outside, dogs (knuckle bones). Then they tossed some bones and, depending on how they fell, the player had to part with some of his "house bones" or, if the toss was good, received additional bones from other players. The order of importance in which bones were surrendered was, perhaps, indicative of value judgments long ago: first women; then house parts; then some dogs; the rest of the house; and, finally, the rest of the dogs. If men were lost, the game was lost.

Ekalun of Bathurst Inlet loved to gamble, but since he rarely saw other people, he had few opportunities. When the chance came, he and his friends played cards. In the past, he once told me, they also played an Arctic version of roulette. The players sat in a circle. In the center on a piece of ice or hardened snow stood a gracefully carved ladle of musk-ox horn. The players placed their bets, the fur-clad croupier pronounced the Inuit equivalent of *"Rien ne va plus!,"* spun the ladle, and he to whom the handle pointed when it stopped was the winner.

In a painful game of strength that I've often watched but always avoided, two men link index fingers and try to pull the opponent's hand and arm across a line. (In Germany it's called *Hakeln*. Brawny Bavarians like to play it, especially after they've had a few beers.)

Much more fun is *ajaqaq*, the still-popular cup-and-ball (or ring-and-pin) game, the ancient *bilboquet* of Europe. Once, in the intensely religio-magic world of the Inuit where all humans and animals had souls and inanimate things had spirits, it was believed that the ajaqaq game hastened the return of the sun, and it was consequently primarily a game played in winter and early spring.

A huge piece of Styrofoam makes a marvelous teeter-totter for Erika and Dennis Aviugana.

A tug-of-war at the 1966 spring festival in Igloolik, northernmost Hudson Bay.

In its simplest form, ajaqaq consists of a short piece of hollow bone to which a pointed stick is attached by a short sinew string. One flicks up the bone tube and tries to impale it on the stick. Done by an Inuk with plenty of practice, it looks ridiculously simple. Samson Koeenagnak of Baker Lake, west of Hudson Bay, with whom I lived at Aberdeen Lake, then one of the last camps on the Barrens, succeeded, on the average, nine times out of ten. On my first try I had about fifty misses before achieving one solitary success.

In more intricate forms of ajaqaq, a seal or bear carving into which many holes have been drilled is used. Since some holes are easy to hit and others very difficult, a whole scoring system goes with these variations of the ajaqaq game. Naduq of the Polar Inuit, Inuterssuaq's wife, was marvelously skillful. She and Inuterssuaq often had visitors and after supper we sometimes played with a beautifully carved ivory ajaqaq with many holes and a very short string. By then I had spent days in training and was fairly good at the game. The Inuit always scored higher, but when Naduq's turn came, she never missed. Her kindly, deeply lined face crinkled in concentration, her eyes shone, she flicked her wrist, and each time the ivory pin hit one of the most difficult holes.

The manual dexterity and tremendous visual memory that outsiders so admired among Inuit were honed, since childhood, by many games of skill. Games also sharpened other abilities. "Both

children and adults are often superb mimics, wonderfully imitating someone to the delight of all," noted the ethnologist Edmund Carpenter in the 1940s. "I have seen 'take offs' that would do credit to professional comedians; children especially seem gifted in this line." Later, as hunters, some of these children would use their acting skills, their ability to imitate, and their knowledge of animal behavior to successfully stalk and kill seals and caribou.

At Bathurst Inlet, three-year-old Karetak, the son of George and Jessie, was our camp comedian and an expert mime. "How does the white man eat his meat?" one of the adults asked, and Karetak, delighted to be the center of attention, went through a very funny pantomime of me. He pretended to take a chunk of meat, bite into it and cut off a piece, close to his nose, very cautiously and with cross-eyed concentration. All laughed and then, egged on, he would parody someone else. It was amusing and never mean, "an innocent source of merriment."

Children copied in play form the activities of adults and thus acquired some of their knowledge and skills. Boys shot with small bows, made by their fathers, at targets, or at snow buntings or sandpipers on the beach. Girls mothered dolls and sewed small garments for them. Both boys and girls played "home," often with striking realism and attention to details. At the Aberdeen Bay soapstone-quarry camp on the south shore of Baffin Island, I watched two children set up house: a pudgy, busy boy of three and an efficient, well-organized girl of four. A circle of pebbles formed the outline of their home. He brought in "food" and sleeping robes (an old blanket). She lit the pressure stove (an empty can of camping fuel), pumped it frequently and then made "bannock" with kneaded mud and "baked" it in a "pan" (the old lid of a kettle). He parked a snowmobile, in pantomime, then came in, they "ate" the bannock, drank "tea," nuzzled fondly, pulled the blanket over themselves, and "made love."

In 1929, the scientists Therkel Mathiassen and Frederica de Laguna excavated, layer after layer, an ancient Inuit midden on a small island north of Upernavik on the northwest coast of Greenland. They found "101 dolls... more dolls than specimen of any other type — and the other children's toys mirrored the culture of their parents so fully that we could have learned the essential character of this [Thule] culture if only the toys had been found. Some of the toys were small implements which children could have used; others were miniature articles... harpoons, bows and arrows, bird darts, lances, bladder darts, sledges, kayaks, umiaks, knives, snow shovels, adzes, mattocks, cooking pots and lamps, meat trays, spoons, platform mats... Anybody could see that the parents loved their children and delighted to make toys for them."

Some toys were ingenious and intricate. Nuligak, a Beluga Hunter, recalled the puppets of his youth: "The aged people who made them would work only at night, being careful to avoid being seen by children. There was a great variety of these puppets: white bears, brown bears, foxes of all colors, weasels, ducks — and to think that all of them moved as though they were alive!" In the large communal winter hall, in the soft yellow light of seal-oil lamps, the children watched in open-mouthed wonder as "a swan hopped over the door sill. It walked into the middle of the floor, stopped, fluttered its wings… looking here and there, stretching and bending its long neck." The puppets were activated by a complex system of baleen springs. The old people died in the terrible epidemics that swept away most of the Mackenzie Inuit, and with them died the ancient knowledge, handed down through untold generations, of how to make these ingenious baleen-spring puppets.

Much else has died: the spirit of the camps, the harmony, the seamless flow of life and knowledge from generation to generation, the sense of belonging, the pride of achievement.

At the Aberdeen Bay summer camp where men from several settlements mined soapstone and women kept home in their tents, the small children amused themselves, but the teenagers, torn away from television and favorite village hangouts, were bored out of their minds. They knew no games. They had no toys. Nothing interested them. Most slept till noon or later, had bannock and tea in bed, and then wandered disconsolately and bored from tent to tent. At night they came to life, but night life at Aberdeen Bay was very limited. I lived in a plywood shack upon the beach, the graffiti center of the camp, and at night the kids mooned about, smoked lots of cigarets and a bit of pot, and told me all their miseries: "We're bored," they said. "We're really bored. There's nothing to do." Among all the phrases on my hut starting with "f," someone had printed with spray paint in large yellow letters: "THIS PLACE IS A REAL BORE" and another disgruntled soul had scrawled beneath it "RIGHT ON!"

Inuit string out across Baker Lake for a game of tug-of-war.

CHAPTER SEVEN

ISLAND BETWEEN TWO WORLDS

Children sit on a hill overlooking the shore of Little Diomede, Alaska. Beyond is Big Diomede Island in Asia.

FOR YEARS I WANTED TO GO TO LITTLE DIOMEDE, THAT STRANGE island between Siberia and Alaska where, I had heard, Inuit still use umiaks to hunt walruses among the drifting pack ice of Bering Strait. Now, in April 1975, I was on my way in a plane from Nome, Alaska, full of cargo for the settlements of Tin City, Wales, and Diomede.

It was cold and clear, the sky a hard metallic blue, the snow and ice beneath blank white. Bill, the pilot, talked of flying in Alaska, and about the Diomeders. He did not like them. "They're rough," he said. "They drink a lot and fight." As we approached Tin City, the plane, pushed by powerful katabatic gusts, plunged suddenly, and whirling snow wiped out all vision. A moment later I saw the rock wall of a cliff directly in front of us, and in a sharp, abstract flash I knew "now you will die" and had an instant of intense regret. Not fear. There was no time for fear.

Bill pulled the plane up; we hit belly on and hung suspended for a long second like a great butterfly pinned to the rock. Then the plane slid down the cliff, scattering parts and cargo. It fell 200 feet (60 m) and stopped abruptly in deep snow. After the screech of tearing metal, it was eerily quiet.

A rescue helicopter found us quickly and took us to hospital in Nome. I had torn my pants and gashed my thigh climbing out of the mangled plane. Apart from that we were fine. "Your blood pressure is high," a doctor said.

Four days later, in a different plane, Bill and I flew again to Diomede. He flew high this time, both hands upon the wheel, the knuckles white with tension. We did not talk much. Bering Strait, beneath us, was a chaos of ice floes and open water, a Jackson Pollock painting in stark black and white. We circled Little Diomede Island, a gaunt dark pinnacle in an icy sea. Three miles (4.8 km) to the west was Big Diomede Island in the Soviet Union and, in the distance, the coast of Siberia. On the northwest coast of Little Diomede I saw the village of Ignaluk, tier upon tier of weather-gray houses tacked to the mountain slope. Bill landed on firm ice near the island, people came down to pick up parcels and left, the plane took off and my luggage and I were alone on the ice.

A Diomede islander catches an auklet using a long-handled net similar to the one used by the Polar Inuit to catch dovekies.

I went from house to house, trying to rent space. Most people were coldly indifferent, a few were hostile. At one home many men were drinking. They said no, but as I reached the door one said: "Go and stay with Alex. He has lots of room," and all chimed in, "Yes, go and stay with Alex." Someone even showed me the house, high on the slope at the edge of the village. Alex was in his early sixties, stooped, sparse gray hair covering a deeply indented skull. He drooled a lot and was hard to understand. But he was friendly and agreed immediately to rent me a corner of his room. I brought up my bags, made my bed on the floor, and was happy. I had a home.

At 2:00 a.m. I awoke with a start. Alex knelt on my chest and shook me violently. "Lasa," he panted. "Lasa," and drooled copiously. I rolled free and got up in a hurry. After much gesticulating, I finally understood that he wanted my razor. Alex wanted to shave. Reluctantly I got my razor out, boiled water, and, while he shaved, had tea. Then Alex had tea and went to bed.

Next day at 3:00 a.m. Alex knelt again upon my chest like a slavering incubus. "Tea," he said urgently. "Tea," and with each explosive "TEA" he spattered me with saliva. I got up and made tea. I understood now why Alex lived alone.

After four nights of Alex on my chest and coping with his midnight yearnings, I had had enough. Attached to the unused church, buried by snow, was a room that was sometimes used by visiting priests in summer. I dug a path and moved in. It was cold but quiet. Later a villager told me the story of Alex. When he was young, the Diomeders lived in troglodytic stone houses, the roofs of logs and sod, built partially into the mountainside. Each house had a skylight made of scraped, translucent walrus intestine. Playing children raced across the roofs. One day Alex stumbled and fell head-first through a skylight onto rocks far below and, said my informant, his head looked like "a ripe melon that's been dropped. They took him by umiak to a famous shaman on the Siberian side. He did a real good job on the outside of the head, but there's something wrong with the inside."

Slowly the village accepted me. Robert Soolook, a hunter in his early fifties, dropped in for tea and talk. "Can you eat Eskimo food?" he asked (Alaskans don't use the term *Inuit*) and, assured that I could, said, "Come for supper." It was a typical Diomede meal, mostly traditional, varied and healthy: walrus meat from last year, preserved in a permafrost "meat hole" in the mountainside, with seal oil, greens preserved in seal oil, boiled bearded-seal intestine with seal oil and onions, yellowish blubber marinated in seal oil, followed by tea, canned apricots, and homemade bread.

After supper, the talk turned to shamanism. The shamans of Little Diomede had been famous, and the last of the great *angakut* of Diomede, Assikassak, who died in the 1940s, was perhaps the most famous of all. "My dad was a real good Catholic," Robert Soolook said, "and he didn't like the shaman. One day the shaman came to our house to borrow something and he and my dad got into an argument. My dad said, 'Oh sure, you can do your fancy tricks in the dark *kasge* [the community hall] but I bet you can't do them here.' The shaman just sort of looked at him, took off his

Tom Menadelook (left) watches as his crew loads the umiak with walrus meat and ivory.

*Tom Menadelook, Jr.,
hunts auklets with a
slingshot.*

parka, took my dad's great skinning knife, the one we use to
butcher walruses with, held the handle in both hands and pushed
that long knife into his stomach. He turned it in his stomach and
some blood flowed and we all stood around and were very quiet.
He pulled out the knife, the wound closed and the blood stopped
flowing. He put the knife on the table, put on his parka and left. I
remember we all stood there, saying nothing. And then my dad
picked up the knife and there was blood on it."

More planes arrived, some with liquor. One of the pilots was
German and we talked in German on the ice. "How many people
live on Little Diomede?" he asked. "I don't know," I said.
"*Hunderteinundzwanzig,*" said a voice behind us. I turned,
surprised. It was Tom Menadelook, one of the island's four *umialit*
(umiak captains) and the mayor of Ignaluk. "Where did you learn
German?" I asked. "In Heidelberg," he said. "I was there for three
years. In the army."

Tom was short but stocky, decisive and curt, a strong and strong-
willed man who drove himself and his crew with remorseless energy
and daring. He was gruff but not unkind. "How's your room?" he
asked. "Cold!" "I've got a shack," he said. "You can rent it. There's a
stove inside. I'll get you a cot." He turned and walked away.

I loved the shack. It was small and smelled of old motor oil and
blubber, but it was warm and it was mine. Once they knew I liked

their food, the Diomeders were endlessly hospitable and I spent many evenings at one house or another, eating, listening, talking — fascinated by their stories, by the history of this strange village that had clung so tenaciously to this hostile rock for more than 2,000 years.

Trade across the strait was very ancient: ivory to China, metal objects to America. As the men in the middle, the Diomeders were ideally placed to exploit and control this ancient flow of goods. For people having the superbly seaworthy walrus-skin-covered umiaks (a 40-foot [12-m] umiak can carry more than forty people or 5 tons [4.5 tonnes] of cargo) the trip across the 57-mile (91-km)-wide Bering Strait was easy.

But this was also a region of war, and trade was often interrupted. Of all Inuit, noted the Russian scientist Peter Simon Pallas in 1780, the Diomeders were the most "warlike," and the anthropologist Edward W. Nelson of the Smithsonian Institution wrote in 1899 that, "in ancient times, the people of the Bering Strait were constantly at war with one another, the people of the Diomede Islands being leagued with the Eskimos of the Siberian shore against the combined forces" of Inuit along the American side. Occasionally alliances changed, and Little Diomeders fought on the American side against their erstwhile allies in Asia. In 1926, when Diamond Jenness dug at Little Diomede, one of the most common artifacts he came upon (still found now) were rectangular ivory plates, once part of the warfaring Inuit's imbricated body armor that, in design, was similar to armor worn centuries ago in China and Japan.

Under Russian rule of Alaska and, subsequently, American rule on the Alaskan side and Russian rule on the Siberian side of Bering Strait, warfare gradually ceased and trade increased. Even the rise of the Red Star over Siberia did not change this. The Diomeders blithely ignored politics and borders, sailed to Siberia in their umiaks whenever they felt like visiting friends and relatives, and collected greens and berries on Big Diomede Island.

This happy if somewhat anachronistic state of affairs came to an abrupt end in 1948 when the Cold War reached the Diomedes. The Iron Curtain clanked down and two boats from Little Diomede were caught on the wrong side of it.

That summer eighteen people from Little Diomede in a happy holiday spirit sailed to visit their neighbors on Big Diomede Island only to be arrested on arrival. They were confined for fifty-two days, interrogated at length, and fed black bread and watery cabbage soup, a drastic change from their usually copious fat-meat diet. They were released only after repeated protests by Washington, and returned home famished and furious. Several men joined the National Guard, prompted more by pique than by patriotism.

For nearly a quarter-century, the separation was total. And then,

one morning, while I lay on my cot and read a book, a galvanizing yell ran through the village: "The Russians are coming! The Russians are coming!" Far in the west two dark dots, barely visible through the grayish veil of wind-driven snow, came toward us across the ice. Half the village piled pell-mell onto snowmobiles and raced out to meet the visitors. They were Victor and Volodia, two blithe spirits in voluminous parkas and beautifully made sealskin pants, sent from a Siberian *sovkhoz* (State farm) to trap arctic foxes and hunt fresh meat, on a contract basis, for the Russian border guards stationed on Big Diomede.

The visitors spoke Yupik, the dialect of nearly all of Siberia's roughly 1,500 Inuit, so different from the dialect spoken on Little Diomede that they could barely understand each other. I unpacked my rusty Russian and was instantly in demand as interpreter. The border guards, they said, had given this meeting their reluctant blessing (both had left wives and children as hostages on the mainland). Détente, of sorts, had come to Diomede. In two days, they promised, they would visit Ignaluk.

That evening I passed the armory, the National Guard building, and saw Tom inside. "What's up?" I asked. "I'm going to call the army and tell them the Russians are coming," he said. That ought to be interesting, I thought, and waited. Tom got a startled captain on the line and, within minutes, a general. "How many Russians are coming?" asked the general. Told there were only two and that, in fact, they were not Russians but Inuit hunters, he said immediately: "That's fine. No problem. Give them a good time," then added, as an afterthought, "perhaps you can find out from

Walrus hunters haul their umiak to the floe edge.

Walrus meat dries on wooden racks on Little Diomede Island.

them what sort of military stuff they've got on the Siberian side." Tom explained the dialect and communications problem and said: "We've got a Canadian here who speaks Russian. Perhaps he can do it." There was a pause and then the general said: "I think I would like to speak to that person." He knew my books, that helped. Would I pump some information out of the visitors, he asked. "No, general," I said. "That's not my line." "Forget it," he said. "It was just an idea. You all have a good time."

In a hard-drinking village, it was the party of the year. Victor and Volodia came with bottles of vodka; earlier that day a plane from Nome had arrived with cases of whisky. The large room was packed with pushing, shouting people, all of them drinking and smoking. "Ask them… tell them… " — everyone wanted information about relatives and friends on the Siberian side. "Drink up! Drink up!" they shouted. I have a low tolerance for liquor; it did nothing for my Russian, which slurred and blurred together with English, Yupik, Inupiaq — a whirl of noise, of languages. The temperature soared. "Tell them!" Sweat-dripping faces gleamed in the fug. Some time during the night I staggered home and collapsed upon my cot. The next day did not exist. Volodia appeared briefly in my shack, barely able to stand, and insisted I send him a book. Tom drove both men to the border and they lurched across the ice toward Siberia. (After I got home, I sent a book. A year later I had a letter from Volodia: the book had just arrived. Lots of censors must have read it.)

The ice between the islands began to break up. No more planes came, no more liquor. The boozy, often violent parties stopped. The four great umiaks were hauled to the floe edge. The hunting season started; from now on the boats would be out day and night. They returned to unload and headed out again. June, on Diomede, is called "the month when people do not sleep."

Weeks earlier I had asked Tom whether I could join his crew as a nonhunting member. He knew I would ask and was brief and

The skin of a newly covered umiak glows golden yellow.

decisive: "Yes. You pay for gas and oil like all of us." He gave me one of his rare smiles. "And you get no ivory," he said. For ivory was what this was all about. Walrus meat and fat were important, the main food of the Diomeder. Walrus skins were needed to cover the umiaks. But ivory was the standard of Diomede economy, their only wealth, the basis of their cherished independence. Most men and many women were excellent carvers. Ivory and ivory carvings were, to some extent, the island currency: people paid for groceries and heating oil with ivory carvings, used them to settle telephone bills, and bought cards with them on bingo nights. A thousand years ago they traded ivory, via intermediaries, to China. Walrus ivory, some from Diomede, was used to make sword and dagger handles in seventeenth-century Persia and Turkey. Now their ivory carvings were sold for tourist dollars in Nome and Anchorage.

In mid-May at 4:00 a.m., Tom, in passing, banged on my shack and I was up and going. I had been sleeping fully clothed, for Tom had said: "We wait for no one." (They didn't. Once two members of our crew, Tom's cousin and his brother-in-law, were just a little slow, and we were a hundred yards [90 m] from shore when they arrived. It would only have taken a few minutes to turn around and pick them up, but Tom kept going. We waved an ironic good-bye, and the two men lost that day's share of the hunt.)

Inuit hunters from Siberia and Alaska try one another's guns on their visit in 1975.

There were thirteen people in our boat: eleven hunters, Tom's eleven-year-old son, Tom, Jr., called "Junior" by everyone, and I. As respectively the youngest and the most useless members of the crew, Junior and I sat on the large grub box in the stern where we were least in the way and least likely to get shot. The men treated us with a nice mixture of solicitude, badinage, and camaraderie. They taught us the lore of the pack, the signs that presage storms, the ways of the walrus. They chaffed us for our fears and clumsiness, but watched that we did not get into trouble. Above all, they used praise to bolster our pride. When it got very rough, in storm and sleet and icy spray, one man said to another, loud enough that we could hear it, "Junior's really tough," or, about me, somewhat more ambiguously, "He's not as bad as I expected," and, of course, Tommy and I glowed in their praise and resolutely suppressed all secret yearnings for a warm bed back ashore.

In the umiak we reverted to an earlier life and, as if reflecting that, the men who, in Ignaluk, always spoke English, usually spoke Inupiaq in the boat. We lived with the currents, the wind, and the ice. We traveled far in search of walrus. A storm hit us among the ice and we were caught in a maelstrom of turning, churning floes of the wind- and current-driven pack ice. The men leapt in and out of the boat and poled and hauled the umiak through cracks between the crashing, grinding pans. Broken floes rasped against the walrus-skin cover of the boat, the flexible frame buckled but did not break. When we reached a stretch of open water, Tom gunned the 40-horsepower motor and raced toward the largest floe. Our bow hit the floe at full speed and all, except Tom, jumped from the rearing 30-foot (9-m) boat and pulled it down and forward onto the safety of the floe, and upon it we drifted safely northward toward the Chukchi Sea.

It was a wild night. The storm screamed across the pack, the ice floes groaned and turned and creaked, black clouds scudded low across the sky. The men made a windbreak out of tarps, boiled a big pot of *kauk*, year-old walrus skin, fatty, crunchy, and energy-rich. They drank lots of tea with it, smoked, then curled up on the thwarts and went to sleep. The storm raged on, they did not care; this was their world, and they felt at home within it.

The Diomeders were always a tough, independent, intractable lot. In 1732, the Russian government sent Cossacks to survey the island and to collect *yasak*, or tribute. "Our attempt to land was resisted by a shower of arrows," the senior surveyor, Mikhail Gvozdev, reported to his superiors. Eventually he managed to talk to the Natives, "but all refused to pay tribute." (To this day Diomeders call a disliked white a *gussuk*, a corruption of "Cossack.") The Cossack Ivan Kobelev landed on Little Diomede in 1791 and found the hundred inhabitants (forty-five males and fifty-five females) healthy, "daring and cheerful." But when early

this century plans were made to build a school on Little Diomede, a preliminary government report warned: "The island is terribly isolated, and the people are hard to handle."

The Diomeders are known for belligerence and reckless daring and have been called "the Vikings of the Arctic Sea," a reputation they rather cherish. One day, two boat crews were in the Alaskan mainland village of Wales and saw a film about Genghis Khan and the Golden Horde, with violence and pillage aplenty. Back on Little Diomede, they were asked by a visiting biologist how they had liked the film. One man grinned and said: "Nothing special. Just a bunch of Diomeders on horseback!"

The walrus hunters in my boat slept soundly, oblivious to the storm. Slowly the wind abated, the sky cleared, the pack spread out, the morning was pure magic. We launched the boat and purred smoothly along dark lanes among the floes, through a fantasy-land of shimmering, wind-and-wave sculptured ice. The ice glowed in the soft opalescence of morning, in delicate lilac, rose, and cool green, and bone-white icicles hung in grottoes of the deepest blue. Thousands of murres and auklets, like dark toy birds, lay scattered upon the satin sea.

Far in the pack we heard the walruses, drifting north upon the floes from the Bering to the Chukchi Sea, all 200,000 funneling through Bering Strait on their annual spring migration. We

Little Diomede hunters search for walrus in Bering Strait.

approached them slowly, cautiously. Masses of madder-brown walruses lay sound asleep in chummy heaps upon brown, dung-smeared floes.

Tom throttled the motor back, the men readied rifles and harpoons. They spoke in whispers; excitement and tension filled the boat. We drifted close to a pan loaded with sleeping animals, and suddenly, upon a low command from Tom, the eleven hunters fired, and fired again and again, a rapid, deadly fusillade. One moment it had been very quiet and then came carnage and chaos.

Dead walruses lay on the floe, fountains of blood spurting and bubbling from the wounds. Others, in fear and fury, poured off the floe like a brown avalanche, rallied and attacked the boat, bellowing with rage, their eyes bloodshot. The men shot onto the water, into the walruses at top speed; most walruses turned and fled. A huge bull, bleeding from many wounds, dived, then shot up and hacked into the boat, and water rushed in through the gash. The hunters were prepared. They stuffed a large piece of blubber into the hole to staunch the leak. Ice and water were red with blood. They shot and killed the wounded walruses and tried to harpoon them before they sank.

Ten walruses were dead. The men pulled the umiak onto the floe, patched the hole, and with amazing speed and precision cut up the 2-ton (1.8-tonne) carcasses. Blood flowed everywhere; piles of steaming guts lay on the ice; men with axes cut heavy-boned skulls to remove the precious ivory tusks. Ivory and a sea of blood; it seemed the essence of the hunt.

We loaded the boat to the gunwales with meat, fat, and ivory, and headed for Diomede. The weather was changing fast. Ragged storm clouds raced across the sky. Gray fog oozed over sea and ice and enwrapped us like a clammy shroud. The wind increased; the heavily laden boat pitched and lurched in the rising waves. They raised the yard-broad waistcloth, furled against the gunwales in calm seas, on paddles and poles around the boat and lashed it securely as a guard against the wind-whipped spray.

The day dragged on toward a dark and evil night. One man stood in the bow to watch for the ice floes that surged suddenly out of the murk and spume and vanished again into the dark-gray void that surrounded us. Tommy and I sat on the food box, lolling against each other with the wildly yawing motion of the boat, shivering and chilled to the core. Toward midnight, when the storm was at its peak, flinging sheets of spray across the waistcloth, and icy water soaked us to the skin, one of the men crept toward us, from thwart to thwart like a huge dark crab, took off his great parka, wrapped it tightly around the boy, gave us an encouraging grin, and crawled back to his seat, now dressed only in shirt and pullover.

We reached Diomede in the morning and unloaded the boat. I

walked slowly up to my shack, made tea and drank it very hot, and fell exhausted on my cot, blood-spattered and reeking of blood and blubber. Two hours later, Tom banged on my shack, I put on my sea-soaked parka, and we were off again.

Days and nights merged. We hunted in fair weather and in foul (mostly foul, Bering Strait is notorious for its storms and fogs). The great racks on Diomede were loaded with drying meat; the ancient meat holes, the deep freezers of Diomede, were crammed with walrus meat and fat. The women worked nearly as hard as the men. Mary, Tom's wife, split walrus skins to be used as umiak covers with her razor-sharp ulu. Their daughter, Eva, eighteen years old and just back from a mainland high school, cut blubber off the walrus skins, and sliced meat and hauled it to the meat holes. Her sister, Etta, a charming, round-faced three-year-old, sat on a rock and copied her mother, Mary, pretending to split a piece of walrus skin with a can lid in lieu of an ulu.

Suddenly, near the end of June, the hunt was over. The last walruses had passed to the north. The four Diomede umiaks had brought back much of the meat and all the ivory of 700 walruses — ample food and relative prosperity, though much of that would be spent on liquor. The men caught auklets with long-handled nets, just as the Polar Inuit catch dovekies. I went with Albert Iyahuk to collect greens on the mountainside; he showed me the many roots, corms, and leaves Diomeders preserve in seal oil and eat with meat.

Tom left to work on the pipeline in northern Alaska. Other men followed, some to the pipeline, some to Anchorage or to "the lower forty-eight." Most went to jobs, some went to jails, usually for brawling in bars. "I spend so much time in the Nome jail, I use it as my home address," one man joked. The Diomeders love to travel, but in fall all flock back to their lonely rock set in an icy sea.

John Iyapana was going with his umiak to the mainland and offered to take me along. Once, in a drunken rage at "whites," he had threatened to kill me. Two days later, sober, he asked me over for supper and was a delightful host, generous, amiable, with an enormous fund of stories about olden times on Diomede. Many villagers were on the beach when we pushed off. "Come back," they called, "come back and bring your family."

RETURN TO DIOMEDE

Fifteen years passed, good years and some hard years. In August 1982, I was on Digges Islands in Hudson Bay with scientists who were studying the murres that nest on the narrow ledges jutting from the sheer, 1,000-foot (300-m) cliffs. They taught me to rappel down these cliffs with 0.4-inch (11-mm)-thick nylon rope. Down was easy, exhilarating, a walk in the void. Up was a dreadful chore, and once I reached the top, I collapsed, sweat-soaked and exhausted, my heart pounding. "You're getting old," I thought

The walrus is the main prey of the Diomede Islanders.

regretfully and paid no attention. I should have. My coronary arteries were badly occluded. Four months later, a few days before Christmas, I had a massive heart attack.

I survived, barely, a badly crippled bird. A multiple bypass operation helped, but the heart had been severely damaged and continued to deteriorate. I still made my northern trips, but where once they had been carefree and impetuous, they were now carefully planned to avoid exertion and stress. My summer with the Beluga Hunters was wonderful, but I tired quickly, was often out of breath, and listened worriedly to the irregular thumping of my heart.

The decline accelerated. In January 1986, Maud and I went to India and Nepal, and it was both marvelous and miserable. We gloried in the ancient cultures, the superb buildings, the land, the people. But I was failing fast and everything became an effort. My lungs filled with fluid, breathing was difficult, my skin turned an unpleasant bluish-gray. We had to hire porters to carry me up temple steps and once, at an airport, I nearly fainted.

By summer, the end seemed near. I walked with great difficulty, one slow, shuffling step at a time. I tried to do research for a book, but found it hard to concentrate. We sat in the garden and read and often listened to music, Mozart for joy, Beethoven for courage.

On July 8, my beeper shrilled, an ambulance rushed me to hospital, and that night Dr. Albert Guerraty, a famous surgeon, opened my chest, took out my heart, now grotesquely enlarged, and implanted the heart of a young man who had died in a motorcycle accident. The first thing I saw when I came to was my hand, and miraculously it was no longer a deadly dull blue-gray, but rosy-pink. I could breathe. I heard Maud's voice in the distance and there was intense joy in being alive.

Ten days of total euphoria were followed by a massive rejection, countered by high doses of anti-rejection drugs that also suppressed my immune system. It became a vicious, debilitating cycle: rejection, infection; more rejection, more infection: pneumonia; aspergillosis, a rare fungal disease that threatened to destroy my lungs; an excruciatingly painful bladder infection; Legionnaire's disease. Each time, there was less strength, less resilience. And some nights, in the sterile gray of my silent room, so weak that I could barely move, I dreamt of going back to Diomede, to life.

After two months, an ambulance dropped what was left of me on our doorstep away from the hospital and more infections. Slowly, very slowly, with the help of Maud and a wonderful team of doctors and nurses, I crawled out of the pit. I walked again, a few yards down the street, Maud holding my arm. In October, we went to Cap Tourmente, downriver from Quebec City, where in fall the fields are white with migrating snow geese. We had been there many times, casually impressed by the clouds of white birds. Now I saw and experienced it all with a new and deep wonder.

Eva Menadelook and me in 1990. She is splitting a walrus hide to be used as an umiak cover.

In January, we were in California to study elephant seals. There are many island colonies and two colonies on the mainland: one at Año Nuevo, north of Santa Cruz and visited by tens of thousands of tourists, the other new, recently discovered on the beach of a secluded cove at the base of a great cliff, known only to a few scientists who kindly shared their secret with me.

Maud stayed at the top of the cliff and I climbed down. I've done a lot of climbing in my life; it was tricky in spots and very steep, but not particularly dangerous. I sat on the beach, watched the great seals and took notes and pictures. After a few hours, I started to climb the cliff slowly, for the implanted heart is not connected to my nervous system; it reacts very gradually to strain and stress. My emaciated arms, stick-thin and weak, could not haul the weight of my body. I rested often. Every step had to be carefully planned. It took every ounce of strength and will, but I made it to the top, sat next to Maud and looked out over the sea, tired but totally happy. For at that moment I was certain that Dr. Guerraty had been right when he promised that, if I survived the operation and its aftermath, I could lead again a normal life, and he knew that to me "normal" meant being in the Arctic, climbing cliffs, returning to Diomede.

I flew to Anchorage, Alaska, in the spring of 1990 and the news was bad. Hunting for ivory had fallen into ill repute. To save Africa's elephants a world-wide ban on ivory trade was now in effect. There had been reports in magazines and in Alaska's press of Inuit "headhunting," of killing walruses only for their tusks, leaving

Children on Little Diomede Island try to catch gulls.

the headless carcasses upon the ice. The more lurid reports spoke of "chainsaw gangs" that lopped off walrus heads. The Diomeders, I guessed, would be very touchy. A Japanese TV crew, I was told, had offered the Diomeders big money to film the walrus hunt and had been curtly advised that they and their money were not wanted. "I wouldn't be surprised," a biologist friend in Anchorage told me, "if they put you back on the helicopter and tell you to fly off."

That was another change: a heliport at Diomede and weekly helicopter service from Nome. It all looked so familiar: the fields of ice in Bering Strait; the soaring cliffs of Diomede; the weather-gray

An umiak in Bering Strait.

houses glued to the mountainside; the umiaks on their racks; the great rust-red tanks for oil and gas. I stared down and worried about my welcome. The helicopter landed on a new metal pad on the beach. There was the familiar smell of sea and wrack and walrus oil. And there stood Tom Menadelook and Mary. He recognized me instantly and was as brief and decisive as ever. "Good to see you back," he said. "Mary and I are going to Portland [Oregon] for Etta's graduation. You can stay at our house." "Junior," he called, and from the crowd around the helicopter came a heavyset, sturdy young man: Tom, Jr., now twenty-six, father of three lovely children, a fine hunter, and the village policeman. "This is Fred," his father said. "He'll stay at our place. Get him the keys. And he'll go out again with our boat." All my worries vanished.

Young men carried the bags up to "my" house. I followed slowly, up the steep, familiar cobbled path. Annie Iyahuk sat on the steps of her house. "Come in," she said. "Albert will be glad to see you." Albert, with whom long ago I had collected greens on the slopes of Diomede, now in his seventies, was thin and frail but still an excellent carver. He grasped my hand in both of his. "Ah," he said. "You came back to us." I was given tea and bread, and hard-boiled eggs with seal oil. After fifteen years, it was like coming home.

There had been many changes in these years: a large new school had been built, a new store, some new houses, a "washateria" owned, like the store, by the islanders and paid for, in large part, with money made from ivory carving. It was kept spotlessly clean and for three dollars one could shower, wash a load of clothing, and dry it. The washateria brought in $100,000 in its first year of operation.

There was one drastic change: Diomede was dry. All alcohol was forbidden. The planes with booze, the wild parties, the fights, the smashed windows, the drunken threats, the bilious hangovers were now only memories of a violent past. "It sure is quiet," I kidded George Milligrock, once one of the wild young men of Diomede and now approaching portly middle age. "Yes," he agreed with a touch of regret, "we're getting to be quite civilized." Young Inuit who had tried city life in Nome, Anchorage, or Seattle and were nearly crushed by drink and other problems, had returned to Diomede, to their roots, to an older, simpler way of life. The population of Ignaluk, after shrinking for many years to a low of 84 in 1970, had increased to 121 in 1975, and to 171 in 1990.

Life on Diomede was peaceful, pleasant, quiet. It certainly was a nicer, gentler place than on my first visit — and yet, some of the panache, the verve, that devil-may-care daring was gone, and at times I felt a certain perverse nostalgia for the wildness of the bad old days.

"Civilization" also seemed to have exacted a bitter price. Once Diomeders had been famous for their daring and their vigorous health. The Smithsonian Institution anthropologist Ales Hrdlicka visited Little Diomede in 1926. "The natives look sturdy," he noted. "None other could survive here." Shortly after I arrived, I met John Iyapana who, on my previous visit, had taken me by umiak back to the mainland. I remembered him as a weather-beaten, bluff bear of a man, violent when drunk, affable when sober, with an immense fund of stories about Diomede. Now he was a broken hulk, wan and weak. He pulled a notebook from his pocket and wrote: "Welcome back, Fred!" Cancer had destroyed his throat and vocal cords; he could no longer speak. He would never tell stories again.

"Long ago, when I was young," said Albert Iyahuk, "people were never sick." Now cancer and heart disease were common; one of the causes may be a partial change to Western food. Recent studies by scientists from the Emory University Medical School have shown "that the incidence of cancer [among Inuit] has increased significantly following westernization."

The shack, my home in 1975, was now full of tools and outboard motors. This time I lived in luxury. Tom's house was large and high on the slope, and in the evenings I sat by the window and watched the sun set over Siberia. I slept in Etta's room, surrounded by posters of rock groups, teen idols, and wild horses. I read many volumes from Tom's extensive library of Arctic books and from time to time, to change from cold to hot, I delved into Mary's collection of Harlequin Romances.

One morning at 4:00 Tom, Jr., stood by my bed. "We go," he said. He was just as curt and gruff as his father and, in many ways, just as kind. We launched the great umiak, eight hunters and I. Of the "old" crew only one man was left — Alois Ahkvaluk, "Big Alois," Tom's brother-in-law, a tall man and immensely powerful. He was quiet and gentle, always friendly and helpful, and during my first visit had a certain fame as the only Diomeder who never drank liquor. One night when Tom, drunk out of his mind, went on a rampage, grabbed an ax and, in berserk, brainless fury, threatened to destroy his boats, I had raced to Alois's house for help. He came, overpowered the raging man with ease, gently took the ax away, and put Tom to bed and waited until he was sound asleep.

The other hunters in the boat were young; some were the sons of my former crew. I sat again on the grub box in the stern, this time alone. Tommy, umialik in his father's absence, steered the boat. The great skin boat surged through the sea, parka-clad men on the thwarts. Gulls mewed, the ice glinted, and far away rose the Siberian coast. Time dissolved, past and present merging; I dozed on my box, warm in the sun, wrapped in the smell and the sound of the sea.

The previous year had been catastrophic for the Diomeders. The weather was bad, the great herds passed, and all four umiaks together took only forty-five walruses. There was no more meat in the village, no ivory, no money. Now they hunted assiduously, but more cautiously than before, avoiding dangerous ice, not going out in storms, and returning home at night to sleep in bed. In a way, this suited me fine. This was soft traveling compared to the past — and yet, foolishly, I hankered for the wild old days, the toss and turmoil of the storm, the screaming of the wind. Now, when the wind picked up, we headed back, beached the boat, and I went home and watched TV, as did all the others.

Still, they were hardy and conscientious hunters, the weather was exceptionally good, walruses were plentiful, and we returned with boatload after boatload of meat, fat, and ivory. The drying racks were once again loaded with meat, the ancient meat holes were full. At first we brought back all the meat and the skins of young bulls and females that, cleaned and split, would be sewn into new umiak covers. Then we brought back only choice pieces of the meat, and finally only token portions — flippers, hearts, and livers — and, of course, the ivory. A horrid waste, the men admitted, but they had all the meat they needed, and without ivory their ancient hunting village could not survive.

On the same beach where I had photographed Eva Menadelook fifteen years earlier, just out of high school and giggly and gauche. Eva, now thirty-three, long married to a fine hunter and mother of several children, split a walrus hide, an exacting skill she had learned from her mother. She sat on a rock, the heavy skin draped over a well-anchored oval board, and with smooth even strokes of her razor-sharp ulu, she split the 2-inch (5-cm)-thick walrus hide into halves of equal thickness. It would take five split skins to cover Tom's 30-foot (9-m) umiak.

Among the women on the beach, splitting skins, cutting meat, talking, laughing, keeping an eye on the playing children, dressed in jackets and jeans, were two nuns of the Order of the Little Sisters of Jesus. I had watched their arrival fifteen years earlier; it was a good example of Diomeder standoffishness. They came by boat in early summer with many boxes and bags. They labored up the snowy path, slipping and falling with their heavy loads, and the young men of Diomede stood by, smoking and smirking, and watched the women struggle. Only Roger Ozenna and I helped, and both later got a ribald ribbing from the young blades in the village. "If ever there was a grim crowd to bring toward salvation," I wrote that night in my diary, "the Diomeders must be it."

Time passed and the nuns — Little Sister Nobu, originally from Japan, and Little Sister Damiène, originally from Alsace, France — became part of the village. They assisted the women with their work, they listened gently to their problems. They were kind and practical, a healing, helping influence in the village, and from time to time, in their spotless kitchen–living room, they spoiled me with delicious meals.

A girl on a sparkling day at the edge of Bering Strait.

In the late 1980s, the world changed abruptly and the Diomeders on their remote rock were caught up in the change. In 1988, Gennadi Gerasimov, a frequent spokesman for Soviet President Gorbachev, flew to Little Diomede, the place, he said "where the West ends." Staring across the ice-bound strait toward the nearby U.S.S.R., he quipped: "This is an ice curtain!" then added, "It really is an experience to see how close we are geographically and still worlds apart in other ways. Let's melt the ice curtain."

It melted quickly. A year later, in September 1989, U.S. secretary of state James Baker and Soviet foreign minister Eduard Shevardnadze met in Jackson Hole, Wyoming, and signed an agreement that would once again permit visa-free travel for Inuit from both sides of the Bering Strait "to see each other as often as they want… and reestablish their family customs and ethnic ties."

The ink on the treaty was barely dry before half of Diomede's large Ozenna clan piled into their skin boat and visited Siberia. Gifts were exchanged. Long-broken friendships were renewed; new friendships were made. Now there were frequent visits, phone calls, and letters. I returned from a hunt, blood-spattered and tired, and walked slowly up the path to my house. Ronald Ozenna saw me,

E P I L O G U E

L'ENVOI

"IN THE OLD DAYS, WHEN PEOPLE WERE DIFFERENT FROM NOW…"
This was the Inuit version of "Once upon a time," the opening
phrase of storytellers.

We sat in his roomy kitchen, an elderly Inuk and I, drank tea,
and reminisced. We had traveled together long ago by dog team,
for weeks and weeks and weeks, and we remembered the good
times and some of the close shaves. We talked of the storms, of the
days without food, of sleeping in the igloo. His five-year-old
grandson listened, half-fascinated, half-bored, and then something
worried him. "Where in the igloo," he asked, "do you plug in the
TV?" We stared at each other and laughed. It was funny and it was
sad; a great gulf separated the generations.

"*Aglani, aglani, aglani*," long, long ago… Thus began every
evening with Inuterssuaq of the Polar Inuit who loved to teach and
tell stories. He told of walrus hunts on very thin ice, of a time when
wood was so rare that the handles of dovekie nets were made of
narwhal tusks, of hunting *nanook*, the great white bear, armed only
with a lance. These evenings and nights with Inuterssuaq were
endlessly fascinating, yet tinged with sadness, because he spoke of a
vanished world.

On little Diomede Island in 1975 lived a lonely old man, David
Kaneveak. He had joined the army during the Second World War,
had drifted to California after the war, and had now returned,
thirty-five years later, to end his days on Diomede. Most of his
friends were dead. He often visited me and talked for hours about
his youth, about "the old days on Diomede," and he gave me
glimpses into a world that was mysterious and strange, for David
Kaneveak was the stepson of Assikassak, the last of the great
shamans of Diomede. He spoke of the spirits that had guided his
father, of the mystic powers he had possessed — of his returning,
dazed, from trance-like trips to another world; of speaking in
tongues that none understood. David Kaneveak was the last link to
the old shaman, to an ancient knowledge that is now lost.

It is an ancient canon that *Natura non facit saltum*, nature does
not proceed by leaps. Charles Darwin was so taken with it, he used
it no less than seven times in the *Origin of Species*. If abrupt change
is unnatural in nature, it also should be so in the evolution of
cultures. For thousands of years Inuit culture evolved, perfected the
art of living in an inimical land, achieved a harmony with nature.
And suddenly, within a few generations, most of it perished. The
ancient, nature-linked culture is being transmogrified into the crass

*Puglik (left) and her
brother Oched (right) wash
the family socks and hang
them up to dry at a
Bathurst Inlet camp in the
summer of 1969.*

materialism of our age, the mass culture of the modern West.

"The past is a foreign country; they do things differently there," wrote the novelist L.P. Hartley. For thirty years I was a part of the past, of this ancient way of Arctic life, where everything was so different, and which is now fading into history. I wrote about it, photographed it, and tried to preserve a portion of the living history of the North.

The past is past, the memories remain: of a fine people, of marvelous trips, of a magnificent land, still wild and free, and I feel like the old Inuk hunter in the poem:

Glorious was life
Now I am filled with joy
For every time a dawn
Makes white the sky of night
For every time the sun goes up
Over the heavens.

— SONG RECORDED IN THE 1920S BY KNUD RASMUSSEN

Opposite: Jessie and Karetak return to camp at Bathurst Inlet.

Below: Trained huskies guide an Inuit hunter to seal agloos, breathing holes beneath the snow.

Polar Inuk Anaqaq Henson is the son of Matthew Henson, Admiral Peary's black servant.

Inuterssuaq, an elder in the Lutheran church, holds a service in 1971 in Siorapaluk, Greenland, the northernmost village in the world.

At the narwhal hunting camp of the Polar Inuit, Ululik Duneq makes a new harpoon of wood and walrus ivory in 1971.

A mother and child in church at Apex Hill, Baffin Island, in 1966.

OTHER BOOKS BY FRED BRUEMMER

The Long Hunt	(1969)
Seasons of the Eskimo	(1971)
Encounters with Arctic Animals	(1972)
The Arctic	(1974)
The Life of the Harp Seal	(1977)
Children of the North	(1979)
Summer at Bear River	(1980)
The Arctic World	(1985)
Arctic Animals	(1986)
Seasons of the Seal	(1988)
World of the Polar Bear	(1989)
Seals (with Eric S. Grace)	(1991)
The Narwhal: Unicorn of the Sea	(1993)